HOW

It was in the Royal Navy during the war that David Cox first came seriously to consider the ideas of both Freud and Jung. After the war he returned to study theology at Cambridge and went on to theological college. Following publication of his book *Jung and St. Paul*, David Cox became a member of the Guild of Pastoral Psychology and is now an Honorary Fellow, as well as having been Chairman on two occasions. The Guild has published a number of his lectures on psychology as pamphlets and in 1970 he was Visiting Lecturer at the Jung Institute in Zurich.

TEACH YOURSELF BOOKS

HOW YOUR MIND WORKS

An Introduction To The Psychology Of
C. G. Jung

David Cox

TEACH YOURSELF BOOKS
Hodder and Stoughton

First published in this Series as
Teach Yourself How the Mind Works 1964
Republished as Analytical Psychology 1973
Republished as How Your Mind Works 1978

Copyright © 1964, 1973
David Cox

British Library C.I.P. Data
Cox, David, b. 1920
  How your mind works. – [3rd ed.] – (Teach yourself books).
  1. Psychoanalysis
  I. Title   II. Analytical psychology
  III. Teach yourself books
  150′.19′54   BF175
  ISBN 0–340–23325–7

All rights reserved. No part of this publication may be reproduced or transmitted in any form or by any means, electronic or mechanical, including photocopy, recording, or any information storage and retrieval system, without permission in writing from the publisher.

ISBN 340 23325 7

Printed and bound in Great Britain for
Hodder and Stoughton Paperbacks, a
division of Hodder and Stoughton Ltd, Mill Road,
Dunton Green, Sevenoaks, Kent (Editorial Office:
47 Bedford Square, London WC1B 3DP) by
Richard Clay (The Chaucer Press) Ltd
Bungay, Suffolk

Contents

7 Psychic Development

8 Archetypes

Foreword

There is no doubt that there is immense value to be gained from an understanding of Jung. But it is a formidable task to begin a study of his psychology from his original works. As a Jungian analyst I am often asked to recommend books which make his ideas accessible at an introductory level. There are few such books, and I do not know of any that gives a fair picture of the elements of Jungian psychology with so much clarity and simplicity as this one does. The author is not himself an analyst, and it is perhaps for this very reason that he is at so much pains to clarify or dispense with technical terminology.

One of the most baffling problems for the layman is to find his bearings among the many different views that appear in the name of psychology. In order to meet this need, the first three chapters of the book define the subject matter of psychology, and outline contemporary theories other than those of Jung. Chapter 4 describes aspects of psychic functioning recognised by most therapeutic schools. Chapters 5 to 9 elucidate the central concepts of Jungian psychology. And the last chapter gives a brief account of the author's impression of analysis.

All good teaching is an art, and bears within it something original from the personality of the teacher. This book is no exception. It has a certain bias. It is more concerned with the nature of man and his need for self-knowledge than with clinical conditions of sickness and health. This approach is a valuable one, because Jung's researches were immensely varied and have a significance far beyond the narrow confines of medical or curative psychology.

It might, however, be of interest if I were to indicate some of the differences of emphasis that are part of my own bias as an analyst. The analyst is in contact with the inner life of individuals over long periods of time, and therefore sees the unconscious mind as a living process which has both continuity and purposiveness. The symbols and symbol-making activity of the unconscious mind are ever-present realities. Conscious mind, on the other hand, has far less power, effectiveness and continuity. It dies every night in sleep, and is modified by conditions of health, fatigue and a variety of other influences from within and without. To the analyst it often seems that the fluctuations of consciousness, rather than of the unconscious, might be described as 'odd things'.

Nevertheless, the mind as a whole has what Jung calls 'psychic reality', which is different from the material reality of the body and the external world, but which is known to exist both because we 'experience' it and because of its effects in the external world.

For practical analysis, dreams are an important part of the reality of the mind. When a dream is rightly interpreted, the conscious mind is enlarged and strengthened by new insights. It is possible that the understanding of a single dream may bring about a transformation of the personality. A series of dreams may be shown to have a continuity of meaning, which is not only helpful to the patient but also suggests that 'meaning' is an inherent characteristic of the human mind. The realisation of 'meaning' requires the co-operation of both the conscious and the unconscious mind.

Jung found that a 'sense of meaning in life' was essential to human health, happiness and even sanity.

At different stages of the life cycle, the content of this meaning changes. In the first half of life meaning is concerned with the establishment of the ego, the fulfilment of biological needs and duties and the achievement of a place in the world. In the second half of life the sphere of meaning shifts to the goal of inner understanding. Not everyone arrives at this stage of understanding. Those who do experience a process of development, which Jung called Individuation. As a result of Individuation, the personality is reintegrated as a unique whole, in which the ego is subordinated to something greater than itself within the psyche. This greater something Jung called the Self.

It will be apparent that the points I have mentioned are all concerned with the mind as it unfolds in the dimension of time and in the life-cycle of the individual. This is the bias of the analyst, who is always confronted with the psychology of a particular individual at a particular time of life in a particular life-situation. The task of the analyst is to help his patient to find the meaning of his life, which has been lost because consciousness and the unconscious are no longer co-operating.

None of these points is neglected by the author. But in his exposition he has subordinated the time dimension to the structural aspects of the psyche. This has been a wise and careful selection, because it has enabled him to present with a remarkable simplicity and clarity a subject which is in fact immensely complex. Anyone who is familiar with the vast range and profundity of Jung's thought will appreciate the nature of the author's achievement.

Faye Pye
B.A. Cantab., M.A.(Psych.), Lond.,
L.R.C.P., M.R.C.S.

1 What is Psychology?

Thought

Psychology is primarily concerned with what goes on in the mind. For example, when someone is afraid, all sorts of things are happening at once and some of them are the concern of psychology. When a man is afraid electrical currents are passing between the cells of his brain and along his nervous system; a chemical substance called adrenalin is being pumped into his bloodstream; he is 'feeling afraid'. When we think about what it means to 'be afraid' we may think about any of these things, and they are all somehow connected together. If adrenalin is artificially introduced into someone's bloodstream it is found that he feels afraid, even though there is nothing for him to be afraid of. Whether what we are doing when we think about being afraid and things like that is 'psychology' or not depends upon what we are thinking about, and upon the way in which we think about it.

It is quite possible for someone to think about fear without thinking about the feeling of 'being afraid' at all. He might simply examine the electrical discharges in the brain and the nervous system, and see how they are related to each other and to the bodily movements of the man who is afraid. A person who thought about fear in this way would not be thinking about it psychologically, because this way of thinking about what happens is called 'neurology', which means the study of the nervous system. Someone else might choose to study the way in which the glands of the body produce adrenalin when we àre afraid, and this would be 'biochemistry', that is the study of the chemistry of living things. We should only speak of 'psychology' when what is being thought about is the actual feeling 'inside' of 'being afraid'—although when one is thinking psychologically one may try to see how this feeling is connected with the brain, the nervous system and the glands. Psychology is concerned with what goes on in our minds, and we should always remember that this is different from what happens in our brains. The things with which psychology is concerned are things like fear, thinking, hoping, making decisions and so on.

Behaviour

Psychology is also concerned with many of the things that people do. If an unarmed man meets a lion he is likely to be afraid, and when someone is afraid he is likely to turn and run. When someone who is afraid runs away from the thing he is frightened of it is obvious that there is some connection between that person's fear and his running away. Just as we can think of being afraid in several different ways, so we can think of its connection with running away in different ways. For example, one can discover how the adrenalin which is produced influences a man's ability to run, or one can wonder what sort of images occur in the man's mind as he runs; the first way of thinking about it belongs to biochemistry, the second to psychology. If one thinks that the running away is somehow caused by the man's fear, or that it is in some way an expression of that fear, then the running away is part of psychology, because the man's behaviour is thought of as the result of what is happening in his mind. In other words, psychology is often about what people do as well as about what they think or 'feel'.

Although psychology is often concerned with human behaviour it is not concerned with all kinds of behaviour. For instance, when a doctor is examining a patient he may tap the leg just below the knee, and if the patient is normal his foot will kick forward. This is known as a 'reflex', and, so far as we know, it is a purely physical response on the part of the nervous system in the region of the knee. It does not appear to be connected either with the brain or with the mind. Reflexes of this kind that are part of the mechanics of the human body are not usually the concern of psychologists— although sometimes there may be psychological reasons which prevent such reflexes from occurring.

If someone trips at the top of the stairs and falls down them, one can examine the ways in which his body fell and the 'mechanics' of his tumble, and this would not be psychology at all. If the head of the staircase was dark and there was some unexpected slippery thing at the top, then it is difficult to see how any study of the fall could be psychological. On the other hand, if the fall occurred in the person's own house, on a well-lit staircase that he had often used, one might well look for psychological reasons for his fall on that particular occasion. These illustrations show how the study of behaviour is often psychology, and also how difficult it may be to see when behaviour should be studied in this way and when it should not. The general rule is that the study of behaviour is psychological when what a person does is done because he is the particular person he is, and not merely because his body is influenced by some kind of force from outside.

Perception

When we speak of 'behaviour' we are inclined to think of things that we call 'actions', things that we 'do' *and know* that we do. There is another kind of behaviour, which goes on most of the time, that we do not often notice. Sitting down, standing up or walking along, we are always taking some sort of note of our surroundings. We notice the chairs and tables in a room, the shops as we walk along the street and the people whom we meet. We do not only do things to the world around us, we also take note of what that world is like. This kind of behaviour is called 'perceiving' or 'perception' and, like being afraid, it is something that we can think of psychologically and also in other ways.

A man goes into his garden in daylight and he sees a red rose. At first we think that this is something very simple, because most of our waking life we are seeing something or other, but when we begin to think about what seems to happen we realise that it is not at all simple. The man would not be able to see a rose or anything else unless light was shining upon it, and we are told that some of the light that shines on the rose is reflected from the rose into his eyes. The light rays falling upon his eyes are focused by the lenses in them and concentrated on the retina at their back: the optic nerve is stimulated by the concentrated light rays and an electrical discharge along the nerve produces electrical movements in his brain, and the frequency of those movements is connected with the colour of the rose that he sees. At the same time, he is aware of what we call 'seeing' the rose, and what he sees is not just a patch of colour but something that he recognises as 'a rose'. When we speak of 'perception' we are speaking of the whole business of becoming aware of a rose—or anything else—and it includes the fact that we distinguish the things we see, as well as that we are aware of seeing different patches of colour.

It is obvious that physics and neurology are both sciences that enable us to think about perception, and that there are many things about perception that are not the proper things for psychology to study. At the same time, the fact that we are aware that we are seeing a rose, for example, is clearly a fact about what is going on in our minds, and so it is something that we must take note of when we are thinking psychologically.

Hallucination

When we think about perception we should also think about hallucination. We say that we perceive something when there is something 'there' and we see it, but sometimes it seems to people that they see something (or hear or touch it) when there is nothing 'there' to be seen, and this is called 'hallucination'. If we are certain that there is no reasonable physical explanation of an hallucination, it is something that we can think about psychologically, because we can ask why that particular person should have come to think he saw the thing he did.

There are some occasions when we seem to become

aware of something that is not there which is not the
concern of psychology at all. The easiest illustration is
that of someone who has had a leg cut off. A person
who has lost his leg still feels pains and cramps and
movements in the toes of the foot which is not there, and
this appears to be simply explained by thinking about
the nervous system. The nerves that carry 'messages'
between the foot and the brain pass all the way through
the body, and when the leg is cut off they are only cut,
they are not wholly removed. Suppose, for example,
the telephone line between London and Edinburgh is
cut at Rugby, and a message is sent along it from Rugby
to London. If the person who received the message at
London does not know that the line has been cut he has
no way of telling the difference between the message
from Rugby and one that has come from Edinburgh;
all he knows is that the message has come along the line
from Edinburgh. In the same way, the nerves from foot
to brain may be cut off at the knee, but they still exist
between knee and brain, and stimulation of those
nerves at the place where they have been cut will
produce the impression of pains and movements in the
(no longer existing) foot.

Forms of Psychology

All psychology is concerned with our thoughts, with
much of our active behaviour and with our perceptions
of the outside world, but there are a very large number
of different ways of studying these things. 'Psychology'
is not one science but a name that includes a great
number of different sciences, all of which are concerned
with the same sort of things. 'Psychology' may mean

thinking about the nature of our mental activities like hoping, wanting and making decisions; it may mean studying the words we use to talk about these things; it may mean a survey of the way in which people actually think or behave; and it may mean the consideration of the way in which people can be helped when something has gone wrong with their minds. In this book we shall be concerned with one special form of psychology, but in this chapter we shall give a brief indication of one or two of the other forms that psychology takes.

Philosophical Psychology

Certain people once said that the only thing anyone ever wants is 'pleasure', and that all desires are desires for pleasure. We are not concerned whether this is true or not, it is simply an illustration of the kind of thinking that can be called 'Philosophical Psychology'. Psychology of this sort is the attempt to understand more clearly the things that go on all the time, which we know about very well but which turn out to be quite complicated when we really start to think about them. Such things include, for example, the business of making a choice or decision. How is it that when we have to decide between several different things to do we choose to do one and not another? How far does our 'sense of duty', our 'conscience' or our moral standard influence us? And how do we manage to decide between doing something that we want to do very much and something that we do not want to do but believe we ought to do? If we say that we are 'free to choose' between alternatives, do we merely mean that circumstances do not force a choice upon us, or do we mean something more than this? If we do what we do because we are the sort of person that we are, can we also be said to have been 'free' to do something different? Philosophers have been asking questions like this for a very, very long time, usually in connection with problems of behaviour, and any study of this kind is psychology.

Philosophy in England today pays a great deal of attention to the way in which we use words, and this has its effect on philosophical psychology. Psychology of this sort may be concerned with what we mean by words like 'fear' and 'hate'. We often talk as though 'hate' were something that a man has inside him, but it is difficult to see just what this means. It can be suggested that when we talk about 'hate' we are simply talking about people's thoughts and behaviour. If John hates Jack, it may be said: 'That means that John speaks in a nasty way when he is talking to Jack, thinks with pleasure of unpleasant things happening to Jack, will not go out of his way to help Jack, may even hinder him and so on—and this is all that we mean by 'hate'. Once again, it does not matter whether this is a true account of what we mean by a word like 'hate', it is merely an example of the sort of thing with which philosophical psychologists may be concerned.

Statistical Psychology

Not very long ago Kinsey produced two large books about people's sexual behaviour. In his introduction he pointed out that before we talk too much about how people ought to behave in connection with sex it would be a good thing to try to find out how they do behave. In order to do this he collected evidence from a very large number of people and arranged the results 'statistically'; for example, he gave the proportion of married men in his sample between the ages of (say) thirty and forty who had sexual relations with women other than their wives. Much statistical psychology is done by means of widespread enquiries intended to find out how people behave or think in connection with one thing or another. The results of such enquiries are arranged in such a way that they show patterns of behaviour—all those who behave in a similar way are grouped together, and this grouping is then compared with other ways of grouping the same people, such as social background, living in town or country, having brothers or sisters, being only children and so on.

The multitudinous tests used for so many purposes nowadays are also part of statistical psychology. Intelligence tests are designed to compare the ability of people to distinguish and relate the material with which they are presented; there are personality tests designed to show degrees of neurosis, or the extent of introversion or extraversion; tests are carried out to compare perceptive ability in normal circumstances with the same ability in special circumstances—for instance, in emergency or under drugs. The field of statistical psychology is as large as the field of human behaviour, and a great amount of work is being done in connection with it. The thing that distinguishes this kind of psychology from most other kinds is that it is concerned with the general or 'normal' behaviour of a large number of people, not with the peculiarities of the individual. In this respect statistical psychology is the opposite of psychotherapy, which is concerned with the problems of the individual and of which we shall have much to say in later chapters.

Behaviourist Psychology

We decide what sort of person someone else is by seeing how that person behaves, and our own behaviour is a very clear indication of what we are. People's behaviour is a good guide to their inner nature, and a study of someone's behaviour may tell us a great deal about what that person is. It may also be said that, for most purposes and from most points of view, what a person does is more important than what is going on in his mind, and that the real importance of what goes on in the mind is the way in which it affects behaviour. Because of this, when behaviour is thought of as an expression of a man's inner nature, there is reason for regarding the study of behaviour as a form of psychology. 'Behaviourism', however, has become the name of a special attitude to psychology, and it is usually connected with a particular opinion which is called 'Epiphenomenalism'.

Everyone must admit that there is some connection between the way a person behaves and what is going on in his mind. If someone sees that the edge of the cliff on which he is standing is about to crumble he will jump away from it, and at the same time he will have a feeling of fright, or an awareness of danger. Some people would say that he sees what is about to happen, realises the danger, feels afraid and, *as a result*, moves quickly away. In other words, some people would say that his (mental) awareness of danger is the cause of his running away. Those who hold the theory called 'epiphenomenalism' deny this: they say that there is a direct connection between the sight of the falling cliff and the jumping away, and that this connection has nothing to do with the sense of danger or the feeling of fear. Such people say that the feeling of fear is something that happens at the same time as the sight of danger and the jumping away, but that it does not cause the person to run away. According to them, jumping away is a reflex action which occurs when the cliff is seen to be about to fall.

The ideas behind this view can best be illustrated by the well-known experiments that Pavlov and others did with dogs. The kind of thing done was to put a dog in a cage at one end of a wired-in run and a plate of food at the other end. When the cage was opened the dog ran to the food and ate. Then the experiment was repeated, and when the food was put in position a circular disc was displayed; at other times an empty plate was put down and a square shown. After this had been done many times it was found that the dog would run out of its cage when a circular disc was shown and stay in its cage when a square was shown, whether or not food was put down at the same time. The natural reaction of the dog to food had been transferred, by a process of conditioning, to the differently shaped tokens, and the reflex response to the tokens was known as a 'conditioned reflex'. The idea of a 'conditioned reflex' is used by behaviourists to explain the great majority of human actions.

Most of us do not think that the ideas of behaviourists are satisfactory, but although we may not be ready to think that all human behaviour can be explained in terms of reflex action to the situations in which we find ourselves, it is as well to realise that a great deal of behaviour can be explained in this way. Children who have become accustomed to the way their school is run do not need to stop and think when the bell is rung after break: they simply move towards their classrooms, and this is a reflex action to the bell. We do not think about cleaning our teeth every night, but at a certain stage of the business of going to bed we reach for our toothbrush.

The attitude of behaviourists can be illustrated in practice by the example of a psychologist who devised a cure for writer's cramp. Writer's cramp is the inability to hold pen or pencil in order to write with it, and the assumption was made that this was the result of some unpleasant experience associated with writing. The object of the cure was to 'uncondition' the reflex by associating something equally unpleasant with failing to write. In order to do this a simple apparatus was designed: the patient attempted to trace out lines or letters with a steel instrument held like a pen, and when he failed to trace them correctly he received a sharp electric shock. It was claimed that this apparatus did, in fact, produce satisfactory results and made people suffering from writer's cramp able to write freely again.

Therapeutic Psychology
All the forms of psychology of which we have spoken are concerned with examining or thinking about the way in which people think or behave. It may be that, as a result of such examination, suggestions can be made that may help people to overcome difficulties of thought or behaviour (as we saw in the case of the attempted cure of writer's cramp, based on the theories of behaviourist psychology), but if this does happen it is more or less accidental. The aim of all these forms of psychology is more accurate knowledge about the way our minds work and the way in which we behave. The kind of psychology with which we shall be concerned in

the rest of this book is concerned with the actual problems of individuals who need help, and it is called 'Psychotherapy', because 'therapy' means 'healing'. This kind of psychology starts in the consulting room, when an individual patient is seeking healing because of some trouble that has upset his normal living. Such a patient does not want to be told any theories or ideas about psychology, what he wants is real practical help.

Most kinds of psychotherapy have two aspects. On the one hand, there is the way in which the psychotherapist tries to help the patient, that is what actually goes on in the consulting room. This is the first and most important thing and everything else in psychotherapy is somehow connected with it. At the same time, if psychotherapists are to learn more about their work and to benefit from each other's experience, they have to understand what they are doing as well as do it. This means that psychotherapy includes the development of ideas about what is going on during psychological treatment, about the way in which the mind should work and about the way in which it does work. In other words, psychotherapy includes a great deal of theory, and we shall have something to say about this in later chapters.

It is sometimes suggested that psychological theories that have grown out of the attempt to cure people suffering from mental diseases are of little importance to people who are 'normal', but it is easy to see why this view is wrong. The doctor who seeks to heal diseased bodies would be able to do very little if he had no idea how the body ought to work when it was not diseased (for one reason, he would not even be able to tell if his patients were suffering from a disease or not), and much the same is true of psychotherapists. But it is also true that it is by no means clear that anyone *is* 'normal', if 'normal' means 'without any kind of disturbance of the most efficient working of the mind possible'. On the whole it seems most likely that those who are in urgent need of psychological help are suffering from an exaggerated form of a difficulty that occurs again and again in a less violent way in people who are perfectly 'normal'—in the sense of not being noticeably different from a great many other people.

Psychiatry

All psychotherapy has developed from medicine, but there are two main forms, 'psychiatry' and 'psychological analysis'. It is not always easy to draw a line between the two, and it should be said that most psychiatrists make some use of the methods of analysis and that some analysts do occasionally resort to the methods of psychiatry. Psychiatry is more directly connected with the work of medical doctors and is carried out on similar lines.

Although psychiatry is concerned with disorders of the mind, it is very closely connected with neurology, and the psychiatrist often attempts to influence the mind by working on the brain. The two most obvious instances of this are 'electrical shock therapy' and 'leucotomy'. Shock therapy is designed to give a violent disturbance to the brain in such a way that the things that prevent its proper functioning are cleared away; leucotomy is an operation by which various parts of the brain that appear to be causing serious disorder are cut off from the rest, so that they no longer interfere with it—very much as a doctor may feel that it is necessary to amputate an infected limb to prevent it from poisoning the rest of the body. Psychiatrists may also employ drugs, long periods of sleep and other physical means in order to attempt to help their patients. And, as we have said, there are psychiatrists who rely largely on the methods used by psychological analysts.

Psychological Analysis

One way in which psychological analysis differs from most psychiatric practice is that no use is made of physical means. The idea is to deal directly with the mind of the patient, and the treatment could be described as a 'talking cure', because the only really satisfactory way of getting to know the mind of someone else is by talking to that person. It should be added, however, that there are some analysts who are ready to make use of the methods of psychiatry when they think that they may aid the 'talking cure'. For example, an analyst might believe that when it seemed impossible to talk to a particular patient at all some form of shock therapy might make this possible. Analysts do not regard their method as a panacea for all mental troubles, knowing that some patients are more helped by analysis, others by drugs. In general, however, the analyst does his work through talks with the patient.

In the end psychological analysis is concerned with only one thing and that is the patient's knowledge of himself, and in this it is a long way removed from traditional medicine. On the whole what is important in medicine as it has been practised in the past is that the doctor should correctly diagnose the disease from which the patient is suffering and know how to cure it; he may well give the patient a great deal of information about the disease and about the methods of cure, but one does not usually imagine that the success of the cure depends upon whether or not the patient understands what is going on. Penicillin will destroy harmful germs within the human body whether the patient knows anything or nothing about what is causing his trouble, or about the action of penicillin. Analysis is pointless unless the patient discovers things about his own mind that he did not know before, and this is why psychological analysis always takes a very long time.

The job of an analyst is to help the patient to discover things about himself for himself and, like all learning processes, the speed at which this happens depends upon the patient. It is no good for the analyst to keep telling the patient things that the patient is not able to understand or ready to accept: he (the analyst) must patiently wait and watch while the patient gradually comes to understand more and more. At the same time, the analyst should have knowledge gained from study and experience that enables him to say the right thing at the right time—although no analyst would claim to be infallible.

Analysts

At the present time no one has to have any qualifications before he can offer to help people by means of psychological analysis. Doctors have a medical degree, and psychiatrists are doctors who have had psychiatric training and experience, and have achieved quite definite psychiatric qualifications. An analyst may have medical or psychiatric qualifications, but he does not have to have any. Analysts who are not also medical doctors are frequently referred to as 'lay analysts'.

It is obviously not altogether satisfactory for anyone to be able to claim to be a psychological analyst, and attempts are made to prevent it. Analysts form societies and set out strict rules which must be complied with before anyone can become a member of the society—but it must be repeated that it is not necessary to be a member of such a society in order to do the work of an analyst. Two such societies are the Institute of Psychoanalysis and the Society of Analytical Psychologists: the members of the first claim to be following the ideas of Sigmund Freud, those of the second claim to be following the ideas of Carl Gustav Jung. On the whole, the tendency is to encourage would-be members to get a degree in medicine before becoming analysts, but for various reasons the rules normally allow lay analysts to become members as well.

There is one unbreakable rule that both societies insist upon, and that is that the would-be analyst should himself have a full psychological analysis. This is an obviously important rule, and it is not only one that must be kept by anyone who wants to be a member of a society of analysts, it is also a necessity for anyone who wants to be accepted as a responsible analyst by other analysts, whether he is a member of a society or not.

Freud and Jung

Modern psychological analysis was invented at the turn of the century and its early home was in Vienna. It was developed out of the attempts to cure hysteria and other nervous diseases by hypnotism and similar methods which were practised by doctors in Paris. The first work was done by Sigmund Freud and it can be claimed that the basic principles of modern psychotherapy were discovered by him. They were made widely known by such books of his as *The Interpretation of Dreams* and *The Psychopathology of Everyday Life*.

A Swiss doctor, Carl Gustav Jung, was working on very similar lines in the treatment of nervous diseases and he was very impressed by Freud's work. So much so that the two men became colleagues. After a while they found that they could not agree about things that were basic to the work they were doing and they were forced to separate; the result of that separation is that there are now two great schools of psychotherapy, one developing the ideas of Freud and the other those of Jung.

One cannot help feeling that the emotional tension that accompanied the breach between Freud and Jung has resulted in a wider cleavage between the schools of psychology derived from the work of the two men than need have been the case, but, on the other hand, one should not overestimate the gulf between these two schools. There are a very large number of analysts who would not say that they were either 'freudian' or 'jungian' but would claim that they had learnt from the ideas of both men and also from many others. Moreover, many who do claim to be 'freudian' analysts have incorporated many of Jung's ideas into their thought and there are plenty of 'Jungians' who openly acknowledge their debt to Freud and his disciples, in particular to Melanie Klein. Nevertheless, despite the readiness on the part of analysts to learn from both schools and from other analysts, it remains true that there are very marked differences between the two schools, and these differences are clearly shown by the difference in the terms used.

Terms

Suppose two people are looking at a flower garden. The first one is impressed by the formal lay-out of the flower-beds and the grass between the beds and the paths which wind about. He talks about the massed flowers and the dividing paths in terms of the shape of the beds and of their relationship to each other. The other one is interested in the care with which the gardener has arranged the different colours of the flowers, and in the way that they contrast with the green grass and the brown paths. The two people talk about the garden in quite a different way and use different terms to talk about it: the first one uses terms that refer to shape and size, the second uses terms that refer to depth of colour and contrasts of colour. They are both talking about the same garden and they both say true things about the garden, but they say very different things about it. If they go further and each one insists that his way of looking at and talking about the garden is the most satisfactory way of doing these things, then there may be a real conflict between them, even though they both admit that what the other person says is also true (but not so helpful). This is something like the situation in psychotherapy. The Freudians and the Jungians both give different accounts of the structure of the human mind, and their accounts are different because they see different ways of arranging the things that go on in the human mind. The terms they use are different because they bring out the different ways of arranging these things, and each group is inclined to claim that their own terms—that is, their own way of thinking about the mind—are better. The difference in terms does result from a real difference of opinion

The difference between the picture of the human mind given by the two large schools of psychology is so great that a freudian analyst has been reported as saying that he could not recognise any of the features in the jungian account of the psyche, and this makes discussion between people of different schools very difficult. In this book an attempt will be made to explain the terms used by Jungians, but it is as well to know something about those used by Freudians, and in this chapter a few of the main freudian terms will be mentioned and their meaning briefly indicated. The following table is given as a very rough guide: the terms on the left have special meanings in freudian psychology, those on the right have special meanings in Jungian psychology.

Freudian	*Jungian*
Psychoanalysis	Analytical psychology
The superego	The personal unconscious
The id	The collective unconscious
The subconscious	Archetypes
Libido	Psychic energy
	The self

The lists could be greatly extended, but they should be long enough to give most people some clue to the attitude of those who write and talk about psychology: if the terms on the left are frequently used the ideas are likely to be Freudian; if the terms on the right keep coming up the ideas are likely to be Jungian. There are, of course, many other terms which are used by all psychotherapists of whatever school—terms like 're-pression', 'the transference', 'the psyche' and 'the unconscious'.

It should be noticed that in the above table there are only two pairs of terms that correspond: 'psycho-analysis' and 'analytical psychology' are both names for a school of psychology, and 'libido' and 'psychic energy' have very similar meanings; on the other hand, 'superego', 'id' and 'subconscious' provide a way of breaking up the psyche into 'blocks' that is quite different from the way in which it is divided when Jung's terms are used. We shall try to explain the terms common to psychotherapists of all schools and those special to Jungians in later chapters; in this chapter we shall give a very brief explanation of the terms in the left-hand column above.

Psychoanalysis

'Psychoanalysis' is popularly used to mean any kind of analytical treatment, and it is obvious that it would be a very satisfactory word for this if it had not become a technical term. For various historical reasons it has become the technical term to describe analytical work as it is done by those who regard themselves as in some sense disciples of Freud, and it should be kept strictly for use in this way. If we wish to talk about analytical work in general we may have to say 'psychological analysis', or 'depth analysis'. The corresponding name for work carried out by those who are in some sense disciples of Jung is 'Analytical Psychology'. The existence of these two names is an indication of the fact that there are considerable basic differences between the two approaches to psychotherapy.

Superego

The story is told of a man who was drifting down the river at Cambridge and passed by a punt tied to the bank. A man and a girl were talking, and the girl was heard to say 'I don't see *how* I can go out with you if you really do not believe there is such a thing as a categorical imperative!' We all know that there are certain principles that we feel must be respected and that there are strong rules that we impose upon ourselves. These rules are sometimes moral rules, but they are not always moral in the sense of being rules about good and evil. For some people conventional rules have a stronger force than moral rules and a man who regularly cheats at his business might be quite unable to sit down to his dinner unless he was wearing a collar and tie. Sometimes the rules that we cannot break appear to be entirely arbitrary and to have no good foundation at all. A boy was once told that 'you must never hit a screw with a hammer' and it was many years before he could bring himself to do this, even though it might be the most effective way of starting the screw off.

Apart from the rules and principles that we impose upon ourselves nearly everyone also has a picture of the person he is, or ought to be, in his mind and judges his behaviour by the extent to which it conforms to that picture. The rules and principles and the ideal picture of what we ought to be can be thought of as a 'person' inside us who has strong views about how we ought to behave, is always ready to criticise us when we do not behave in the right way and does his best to make us do the right thing or to punish us when we have done the wrong thing. Freudians refer to this 'person' inside us as the 'superego'.

There is no doubt that the things connected with the idea of the superego happen and it is often useful to have a term that enables us to lump them together. In other words, there is no doubt that the term 'superego' does refer to something that goes on in people's lives, but the use of the term means more than this. First of all, by calling all these things 'parts of the superego' one suggests that they form a close-knit group and tend to reinforce one another, and at the same time one also suggests that they are all the same kind of thing. It is by no means certain that this is true. We may feel the force of convention as strongly as we feel the force of a moral principle and we may be guided by arbitrary ideas of what 'must' be done in much the same way as we are by convention and morals, but it does not necessarily follow that they are all the same sort of thing.

The differences between them may be just as important as the likeness. According to Freudian ideas, they are not only alike, they also originate in the same way, and this is the second thing that is meant by using the term 'superego'.

The idea is that as we grow up we take into ourselves ideas and attitudes held by people around us. It cannot always be said exactly why we accept one idea and not another, although some of the reasons are clear enough. If a child loves his mother very much it is quite likely that he will accept, without question, her hopes about the sort of person she wants him to be, so that he takes over from her an ideal picture of himself; if some moral principle is told to a child with great emotional force it is likely to make a lasting impression on him; if certain conventions are accepted by everybody around him without question a man grows up assuming that they must be followed at all times. In such ways as these, it is suggested, a part of the mind is formed that is the reflection inside us of all the people and groups that have contributed to it as we grew up— and this is what Freudians mean by the 'superego'.

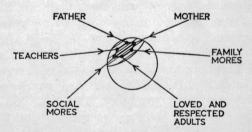

This account of the formation of the superego is an instance of what is called 'introjection'. The idea is that parts of external objects (or images of them) are taken inside the psyche and go on acting within the individual in the same way as they were felt as acting upon him from outside. In the case of the superego, demanding and authoritative aspects of the environment are introjected and they naturally link with one another to form a complex.

The Id

'The id' is the term Freud uses for the raw material of our mental life and it refers to the underlying, instinctive, animal part of our nature. The 'id' contains the driving forces of our life: the desire for food and sexual satisfaction, aggressive tendencies, tendencies to escape danger by flight, or some other means, and so on. The 'id' is said to have no aim but the search for pleasure, and pleasure is said to mean the release of tension—as when we are hungry we feel a sense of strain and tension until we relieve our hunger by eating. The 'id' has no thoughts of right and wrong and no ability to think about things—it can only distinguish between objects it seeks, on the one hand, and those it tries to get away from, on the other. When the 'id' cannot satisfy its desires it forms imaginative pictures of the things that would satisfy them.

All life-force comes from the 'id', but in the course of human development the failure to satisfy all the desires of the 'id' leads to the formation of the 'ego'. This is the conscious mental being that we know ourselves to be and the 'ego' is capable of distinguishing objects, of thinking, feeling, making plans and generally running a life. Whereas the 'id' seeks to satisfy desires directly the 'ego' is prepared to search for ways and means to do so; whereas the desires of the 'id' are straightforward the 'ego' is able to substitute one desire for another. Both the 'id' and the 'ego' are liable to be frustrated by the 'superego', as well as to conflict with each other.

Once again, no one can deny that there are in human beings those tendencies that Freud attributes to the 'id', but to use the term 'id' in this way is to claim that the stuff of our life is of a particular and limited kind—that at the root of human living there is nothing more than the search for the satisfaction of elementary needs that we share with animals and that all else is due to the modification of those needs, or to checks and controls that we have been forced to make as a result of our encounter with the world around. The Jungian view is sharply distinguished from these ideas in that Jung claims that the basic 'stuff' of mental life (that which gives us power and direction) is not merely instinctive and pleasure-seeking but includes strivings towards the 'heights' and is as much related to the most spiritual tendencies in men as it is to the most animal. In fact, some of those things that Freud regards as a part of the 'superego' Jung thinks of as originating in the depths of human nature.

The Subconscious

In ordinary speech it is quite possible to use 'subconscious' as an adjective: we can speak of subconscious thoughts, impressions, ideas and so on. When 'the subconscious' is used as a noun it is a technical term that has a place in psychoanalysis but not in analytical psychology. The Freudian idea of the subconscious can best be described as a dustbin into which we throw all the things in our mind that we do not want—though we must remember that things that have been thrown into the subconscious still have an effect on our lives. They may be out of sight, but they can influence our minds.

The subconscious includes the things one does not want and also the things that one thinks one does not want. This means that there are two very good reasons for trying to do something about the subconscious. The first is that it is not a very satisfactory dustbin, because the things put into it have not been got rid of but are liable to fester and cause a 'nasty smell'. The second is that it is quite possible that we may have made a mistake and that things that have been thrown away are really things that would be very valuable to us if we had kept them. The main reason why 'the subconscious' is not a term used in Jungian psychology is that Jung is concerned to point out that the things we manage to 'lose' are not neatly shut off in a compartment of their own but get mixed up with other things we do not know about and probably never have known about. What this means will be explained later.

The basic 'stuff' of the psyche is the id. When the id is frustrated in its search for pleasure certain parts of it form themselves, or are formed, into the ego. In dealing with the external world the ego comes up against demands, prohibitions and 'laws', and some of these become incorporated in the psyche to form the super-ego. The ego also encounters conflicts and situations that are too much for it, and these are jammed into the unconscious. As a result of these processes, the ego is driven by the desires of the id, inhibited and driven by the demands of the superego, and continually tricked and frustrated by the subconscious. The goal of classical freudian psychology is very similar to that of classical philosophy and scholastic Christianity—that is, to use the power of reason to restrain the unreasonable desires of the id, to free oneself from the overpowering demands of the superego and to cope with the fears that have been thrust into the subconscious. If successful this effort was supposed to lead to a gracious controlled life in which, as one Freudian put it, 'the best that one can say for oneself is that one has not been taken in, even by that "normal psychosis", love'.

Libido

'Libido' means 'desire', with a special reference to sexual desire, and Freud originally used it, with much this meaning, for the drive and power behind human living. In the early days of psychoanalysis he spoke as though our basic drive was entirely sexual and all other aims and desires arose by some modification of this sexual drive. In the development of psychoanalysis this idea has changed considerably and the term 'libido' has lost a great deal of its original sexual meaning. Freud himself pointed out that the sexual aspect of the basic drive *developed* in a person's early years, and this opened the way for 'libido' to be thought of as energy which gradually takes on differentiated forms and becomes directed to specific ends. The term 'libido' is also freely used by Jung and Jungians, but it is used with even less sexual implication. According to Jung, the basic energy of a man (i.e. his 'libido') is bound up with particular aims (of which sex is one, but only one) from the beginning.

The term 'psychic energy' is often used with the same

meaning as 'libido', but when Jung introduced it he was attempting to form the idea of a quantity of energy or power that could be measured and compared, even though it appeared in different forms. In trying to do this he was copying the idea of 'energy' used in physics. In physics we say, for example, that a moving body has a certain amount of energy simply because it is moving and we also say that an electric battery has a certain amount of energy because we know that we can use the battery to light a lamp or run an electric motor, and we can compare the energy of the battery with that of a moving body, even though the *kind* of energy is quite different. Psychic energy is not possessed by moving bodies and electric batteries but by emotions, ideas in the mind, instincts and so on, and in using the term 'energy' Jung hoped that it might be possible to measure the amount of energy that such things have and to compare the psychic energy of, say, a strong desire with that of an ingrained habit. This means that psychic energy ought to be thought of as quantity without quality (i.e. as a measure of how much, not an indication of the kind of thing possessing energy); but psychic energy always appears in the form of some particular psychic drive and this is why the term 'psychic energy' can be used in much the same way as 'libido'.

It should be said again that this brief account of a few Freudian terms is only an outline, intended to give some idea of how they are used and to distinguish them from the terms of Analytical Psychology. It is not only the terms and the ideas that are different, the actual methods and techniques of the two schools are different as well.

Technique

The sharp distinction made in this section between freudian and jungian techniques may, perhaps, have been true once, but it gives a very inaccurate picture of the situation today, especially in England. There has been so much interaction between different schools of psychology, so much syncretism and so much borrowing that the underlying distinctions do not show in obvious ways. Nevertheless, there are underlying distinctions and the simplification made here has a deal of bearing upon them. More on this in the last chapter.

Many people probably have a vague picture of psychological analysis in action. The 'traditional' picture is that of the analyst's couch on which the patient lies in a room with the lights dimmed, while the analyst keeps as far out of the patient's sight as possible. This picture is not true of jungian analysis, but it is largely true of psychoanalysis. Psychoanalysts keep very close to the idea of doctor and patient; in the analysis the problems and difficulties are the problems and difficulties of the patient, the mind that is being dealt with is the mind of the patient, and the analyst remains 'outside' that mind and its problems, probing here, diagnosing there and offering suggestions when needed. The detachment of the analyst is a basic principle of Freudian psychology.

Jung's principles are rather different from this and jungian analysis is based upon the idea that the analytical situation is a personal encounter in which two minds act upon each other. In other words, the jungian psychologist starts with the assumption that he cannot remain detached from what is happening to the patient, and that his own personality influences the patient to a considerable extent. Whereas the freudian analyst attempts to bring his knowledge and skill to the work, the jungian analyst is aware that as well as doing this he is entering into a personal encounter with his patient and that he is not only using his knowledge and skill but also throwing his personality into the work. There is no doubt that this exposes the analyst to many and great dangers, but most analysts (at any rate, most Jungian analysts) would admit that their work is a matter of walking along a knife-edge and they would say that the risk of danger was the cost that has to be paid for doing, or trying to do, anything worth while.

3 Consciousness, the Unconscious and the Psyche

What We Know Ourselves To Be

Before attempting to think about the unconscious it is as well to have some idea of what we mean by 'consciousness', or 'the conscious mind'. We all know what consciousness is, because it is ourselves as we know ourselves when we think of ourselves as mental beings, but it is not at all easy to describe the things that make up consciousness. Any account of consciousness is likely to be a very personal matter and to suffer from the peculiarities of the person formulating it, but this is not of very great importance because other people can correct the errors and omissions by thinking about their own minds. One way of indicating the nature of consciousness is to describe it under five heads:

1 *Life-aims*

A boy may be determined to become the pilot of an aeroplane; a politician may hope and be determined to become prime minister; a young man may intend to 'do the best for himself' and get a job paying good money; a man may intend to make his mark in the world and get fame; another man may aim to be a good respectable citizen, with a wife and family, a pleasant house and an attractive garden; older people may seek no more than to hold down the job they are in, to do effectively the work that lies before them or to 'get the most out of life'. The great majority of people have one or more overriding aims for their life (even if it is no more than to make the best of a bad job), and such general aims as these, which are effective and relevant all the time, are part of consciousness—we know that we have them and we can see how they influence our talk and behaviour, our plans and purposes.

2 Desires

Our life-aims can be described as 'desires', but they have a more general application and are more important to most people than those things that we usually call desires. Our desires are desires for specific things that we can usually get in the near future. A man may like good food, drink, women, going to the opera, playing cricket or sitting by the fire with a good book. In most people's lives such desires take second place to their life-aims and they are not allowed to cause too great an interference in the attempt to bring about the life-aims. For example, a man who aims at leading a quiet, undisturbed, pleasant life may well control his sexual desire for some particular woman if he thinks that, if he did not, his normal way of life would be destroyed. It is often the case that such desires have to be passed by because, if they were satisfied, they would prevent the satisfaction of other desires: if a working man desires to lie late in bed every morning he must not give way to that desire because, if he does, he will lose his job and the money that goes with it.

3 *Habits*

When we desire to do something and then do it we
know well enough what has been going on, but there
are many things that we do without thinking about
them at all. Most people dress themselves correctly
without any thought about what they are doing; many
clean their teeth before going to bed without having to
'remember' to do so; we switch on the light as we go
into a dark room without 'desiring light' and so on.
Desires and habits are closely connected, although not
all habits originate in desires. The difference can be
illustrated by cigarette smoking; some people sometimes desire a cigarette and decide to smoke one, others
simply take one and light one without thinking about it
at all.

4 *Instinctive Needs*

Instincts often give rise to desires and when they do we
become aware of our instinctive needs through the
desires to which they give rise. On the other hand, this
is not always the case and we often provide for such
needs because we know that we must do so, without
having any special desire to do so. For instance, we all
know that it is necessary to eat food and we do this all
our life, usually at regular times; we do not always eat
because we desire food, we often eat because it is meal-
time. Again, most people instinctively attempt to act in
such a way that other people will approve of them and
they know, if they think about it, that they like this to
happen—and yet it would not be true to say that they acted in this way because they had a desire to win approval.

5 *Principles*

Finally, we have principles, and especially moral principles; there are also social principles and conventions. Principles rarely, if ever, point us to some future goal, in the way that our life-aims are directed to some particular achievement. Principles perform something of the function of a hedge, or a fence, or the tracks along which athletes run. Principles can usually be expressed in rules which are either of the form 'Never do such and such' or else of the form 'Always do such and such'. Examples are: 'Tell the truth', 'Do not fornicate', 'Be polite', 'Take off your hat when you meet a lady'.

This list of five kinds of things that we have in our minds is not intended to present any special information about the nature of our minds and it is by no means the only way in which the things in our minds could be grouped. The nature of consciousness is something that each person must find out for himself by considering what goes on in his own mind, but it is likely that most people will find that some or all of these five kinds of things are represented. We also need to notice that, although there is often a collision or opposition between the things in our minds, we usually manage to keep some sort of balance and order between them. We set aside special times and places to satisfy instinctual necessities (e.g. meal-times); we see to it that our desires do not interfere too much with our life-aims; we try to fulfil both our life-aims and our desires within the limits set by our principles; we regulate our life in order to give ourselves leisure in which to satisfy some of our desires and so on. It is also the case that the conflict between things in our minds can set us serious problems:

the businessman may find that his life-aim of getting on clashes with his principles of honesty and truth-speaking; desires may interfere with the fulfilling of a life-aim, or they may clash with one's principles. Such problems as these occur, and so long as we are aware that such a problem exists it is part of what we know about ourselves. We call that part of our mind that we know about 'consciousness', and it is a most important part of what we are. It is sometimes thought that psychotherapy tends to give consciousness an unimportant place and to concentrate attention on the unconscious. This is not true, but it *is* true that modern psychotherapy is concerned with many things that we do not know about in the same way that we know about our conscious mind, and these things are spoken of as being 'unconscious' or 'in the unconscious'.

Dreams

Most people have dreams at one time or another and some people say that everyone dreams, even though not everyone remembers having dreamed. We all know what a dream is and we take it for granted that dreams occur, but we do not always realise how very odd dreams are. One can see that they are very odd by thinking about the way in which we talk about them. When someone begins to describe a dream he says, 'I dreamt . . .' or, 'I had a dream about . . .'. We take it for granted that to dream is something we do and so we use active verbs to describe what happened, just as we use an active verb to say, for instance, 'I hit someone'. But when we dream we do not *do* something, as we do when we hit someone; a dream is not really the result of what we do, it is something that happens to us—it is like being hit rather than hitting, like a brick falling upon one's head. Very few people can say 'I will now go to sleep and dream about such and such', and even those who can do not make the dream, they simply go to sleep and the dream happens. We do not make dreams by conscious thought and yet, somehow or other, a dream is made—the parts of the dream and the images that occur in it are put together in some sort of an arrangement. Where does the dream come from? Here is a dream:

> I was walking along a sea-wall: the wall was very high and the sea on my right was very rough. On my left there was a road running parallel to the wall and I suddenly saw a pretty girl waving to me from the other side of it. The girl started to cross the road and at that moment a red sports car shot into view and knocked her over. The girl screamed and I woke up.

It is easy enough to find the 'bricks' from which the dream was made up. I recognised the sea-wall as belonging to the south-coast resort to which I had been taken for a summer holiday on many occasions when I was a child; the girl looked just like a girl I had happened to be standing next to in a tube train the day before the dream—and she was wearing a dress like one my mother used to have years ago. I had seen the sports car advertised on television a week or two before, and two or three days before a pedestrian had stepped off the kerb in front of me and I had only just avoided an accident. All this was clear enough and yet it was not enough. Each one of these 'bricks' had been wrenched from its context and, somehow or other, been built in with the others.

Working back from the dream it is easy to find the 'bricks', but if we think of it the other way, in the order in which it happened, it is not so simple. We find ourselves asking why those particular bits of incidents from the recent past were selected? What brought up those particular bits from the more distant past? How it came about that they all fitted together into a new shape —the shape of the dream? Why all this trouble was taken anyway? It is clear that a great deal of work has been done: specific material has been carefully selected, it has been taken out of its actual context and rearranged, and then put into a framework in which it did not belong before—and I have no awareness of doing any of these things myself.

The peculiarity of a dream is that we can neither take responsibility for it ourselves nor point to someone or something else that is responsible for it. *My* dream is very much my own dream, and I have that particular dream because I am myself—there are no special rooms such that everyone who goes to sleep in a particular one will have the same dream. The dream seems to have been created by something 'inside' me that I know nothing about, it is something for which I am responsible but which does not seem to have been made by anything that I know of in my conscious mind. Of course, we can often find reasons why certain ideas and images should come into our dreams, but we can rarely explain from what we know about ourselves the way those things are arranged—the pattern of the dream.

Dreams are the most easily recognised instances of a class of things that can be described as 'odd things'.

This is an expression that, as we shall use it, has a fairly strict meaning: an 'odd thing' is something for which we must regard ourselves as somehow responsible but which does not seem to fit into what we know about ourselves. A thing is an 'odd thing' if we cannot show in what way it is the result of something in our conscious mind, or of some force acting upon us from outside. If dreams were the only 'odd things' we might be able to dismiss them as unimportant, but there are very many other 'odd things' and it is impossible to give a complete picture of a man's behaviour without mentioning some of the odd things that occur in his life. Psychotherapists use the idea of the unconscious in order to talk about 'odd things'.

Other Odd Things

A clergyman said, 'On Wednesday I have to go to So-and-So's funeral'—he meant 'wedding'. Weddings and funerals are always likely to be connected in a clergyman's mind because they are both special services for which he gets a special fee, nevertheless there were reasons for thinking that this man probably did regard his friend's wedding as more unfortunate than fortunate. Most of us suffer at some time or another from slips of the tongue and it does sometimes happen that the thing we actually say has an obvious meaning quite different from the meaning of what we intended to say. It can be very embarrassing! Slips of the tongue are odd things that we can talk about by speaking of 'the unconscious'.

Another rather similar kind of odd thing is the inability to remember some well-known name, of a friend, a public character or the author of a book, for example. It is easy to dismiss this as a mere accident, and yet such things happen very frequently and it is found that the idea of the unconscious does help us to understand more about them. Other odd things are obsessive tunes—melodies that run through our head for a day or more that we cannot get rid of. It often happens that we can put words to such tunes and see why they should have come into our head; but, whether we can see why or not, they are odd things.

Most people have some occasion to say, 'I can't think why I did that', 'I wasn't myself when I said that' or 'I do not know what got into me'. A very good example of the sort of thing that makes people say things like this is the quarrel between people who are very fond of one another—often between a courting couple or husband and wife. On such occasions neither wants to quarrel and at the beginning neither says anything that could not have been said (at some other time) without causing any trouble, and yet somehow the antagonism builds up and the two people find themselves in the middle of a violent argument, in the course of which they deliberately try to hurt each other. The expression 'I don't know what got into me' describes this sort of occasion very accurately; it really is as though another 'person' takes charge and makes people say and do all sorts of things that they did not mean to say or do. The sort of thing that goes on might be represented like this:

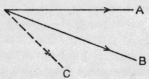

All that we know about our motives and about what we want convinces us that we should move towards *A*, and yet in actual fact we find ourselves going towards *B*. The explanation is clear to the mathematician and the psychologist: there is another force of unknown strength pulling us in an unknown direction *OC*, and our actual direction is the resultant of the force along *OA* (which we know about) and the force along *OC* (which we do not know about):

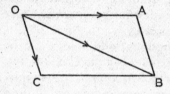

Unfortunately, the mathematician's parallelogram of forces does not help us very much, because we have no way of measuring the strength with which we are pulled either towards *A* or towards *B* and in the parallelogram the lengths of the sides depend upon the strength of the forces—*C* might be almost anywhere in relation to *O*, *A* and *B*; for example:

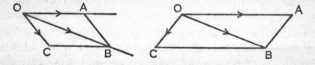

Very similar to this is the sort of thing that psychotherapists call 'excess of affect'. People often find themselves suffering from an emotion that prevents them from thinking or speaking as sensibly as they usually do. They may be overcome by their anger at something that is said, by their dislike of the person who says something, or by love or affection. The oddness of such things lies in the power and extent of the affect, not in the existence of anger, dislike or love: the affect is excessive when it plays too large a part in a person's life at the time. Excess of affect is often connected with political allegiance, so that the mere name 'Tory' or 'Socialist' may prevent a person from forming any rational opinion about what the person labelled in this way is saying. At one time this was also true of religious allegiance, but few people nowadays take their religion sufficiently seriously.

Another group of odd things can be described as 'moods'. The mark of a mood is that it does not seem to have any very clear cause. We simply find that our attitude to everything is coloured in the same way—we may see everything through rose-coloured spectacles, or we may take a jaundiced view of the world. We may just feel that we cannot bear to do any of the things that we know we ought to do and that there is nothing else that we want to do at all. These moods often have some obvious cause, but when we think about it we realise that the effect is out of all proportion to the cause. A letter on the breakfast table bringing some trivial piece of bad news—such as that a friend is going to put off a visit or a member of one's husband's family is coming to stay—may throw one into a mood of sadness for a whole day and one knows that it is quite unreasonable that it should.

These odd things are things that we all come across at some time or another and that we have learned to live with. But although we usually manage not to let things of this sort disrupt our lives too much, they remain 'odd'. We know that they take place, but we cannot really explain why they should and we let them pass, rather than try to get to the bottom of them. In a great many cases this is entirely the right way of treating them, and if there were no other reason for psychotherapy than the existence of such odd things there would probably be no special point in it. Odd things of the kind described above, however, are very closely connected with some forms of mental illness, and the same psychological ideas that help to explain odd things also help the doctor to cope with mental illness.

Mental Illness

The reason why we have called certain things that happen 'odd' is that they possess a double character which involves a contradiction. They are 'ours' and they are things that we do, and yet at the same time they do not happen as a result of conscious purpose and decision. At one and the same time, it is true that we do them and that they happen to us. They all have a quality about them which can be indicated most accurately by the idea of 'possession'. It really is as though it is not we ourselves but some alien power within us that is responsible for our behaviour. This is what actually seems to happen; that is, it is what it feels like when odd things happen—the excess emotion, the mood, the deliberate provoking of a quarrel, is something that we never intended and never consciously caused to happen, but which, nevertheless, happened through us. The idea of the unconscious arises when one carries this way of thinking about odd things a stage further and assumes that there is 'something' within us that is responsible for them and over which we have no direct control.

Odd things occur in the life of nearly everyone and so they provide a useful approach to the idea of the unconscious, but the idea was originally elaborated in connection with the treatment of mental diseases, in which the idea of 'possession' is even more obviously appropriate than it is in relation to more common odd things. In the past a great variety of different names have been used to describe the states of mental disturbance from which people suffer, and the names have changed from time to time. Today the two names in most common use are 'neurosis' and 'psychosis'. The odd things of daily life do not usually cause a great deal of disturbance, but it is obvious that if they were to become more and more frequent, and of greater strength, they would create a serious situation, and we speak of 'neurosis' when odd things occur that do cause a real trouble in someone's life. When people suffer from a neurosis they still have a plan of living and still attempt to order their lives according to their conscious plans and intentions, but they find that their attempts are so frustrated by the occurrence of odd things that they are not able to carry out their intentions. It should be added that they will probably not recognise this themselves but may well put down their experience of frustration to the cussedness of things around them. We speak of a 'psychosis' when a person's life is disrupted to such an extent that he is no longer able to form and carry out clear and understandable intentions and purposes.

Neurosis

When someone is suffering from a neurosis that person knows what he is trying to do with his life and he has a more or less clear idea of how he wishes to enter into relationships with people and things, and yet his efforts somehow fail to 'come off'. He says silly things when he wants to be particularly sensible, he antagonises the people he wants to impress, things 'get on top of him' and he takes attitudes to other people that are quite mistaken. He may feel that people are somehow against him. The ideas people have when they suffer from a neurosis are not absurd, but they are exaggerations of a more reasonable point of view—for instance, the person who is always feeling the need to express thanks out of all proportion to what has been done for him is suffering from a very mild neurosis: his gratitude is not out of place, but it is out of proportion. A neurotic attitude may not be foolish in itself, but it may be inappropriate to the actual situation. A person suffering from a neurosis is usually someone to whom one can talk quite sensibly and, if he will try, he is able to get quite a good picture of what is happening to him. In other words, such a person has a conscious mind that is reasonably well organised but, at the same time, is not able to cope with all that goes on and is liable to lose control over his behaviour.

Psychosis

A neurosis is a disturbance of the mind that makes it very difficult for a person to cope with life and its problems, and a neurotic person is only too well aware of difficulties with which he is confronted, even if he fails to realise that they have their origin in himself. A psychosis is a disease of the mind, and if a person is suffering from a psychosis there are periods when he is not in touch with the world in which he lives. Psychoses are sometimes associated with a physical degeneration of the brain.

Psychoses are of many different kinds, but they all involve a collapse of the personality in the face of the real or imaginary problems with which a man is confronted. For example, a psychotic person may not seem to be *a* person at all: his attitude to people and things may shift violently from one extreme to another, so that at one moment he feels surrounded by friends trying to help him and the next those same people seem to him to be trying to do him down as hard as they can. Each time one meets him his opinions may be different and his plans and intentions may vary from day to day or hour to hour. His inward life may be carried on amid a flood of extraordinary ideas and fantasies which he cannot distinguish from reality. Other forms of psychosis involve more or less regular changes. At one time a person is plunged in absolute gloom, he is beset by a sense of misery and despair, life seems empty and meaningless, and everyone and everything seems to be against him. At such times the feeling of depression fills the whole mind, and in this it is different from a depressed 'mood', because in a mood of depression we recall other times that were not so 'black', we know that there are bright places in the world and we can often take steps to throw it off. When this state is psychotic a person cannot believe that there is anything anywhere except the blackness in which he finds himself. Such a depressed state (in a psychosis) may be followed by a period of apparent normality during which the person is able to cope perfectly well with the problems of normal life. Later the opposite state may occur and the same person may behave with exaggerated excitement, take no thought for the opinions of others or for convention and appear to have no worries in the world; to such a person the normal limitations on human life seem to have no existence.

In all forms of psychosis the effect made upon other people includes a feeling of uncertainty about who the person suffering from a psychosis is. Either one does not seem to be able to 'get at' the person at all, because his whole life seems to be carried on inside his own mind, or one never seems to meet more than a small part of him and seems to meet a different part from one moment to the next, or the character of a person seems to swing from extreme misery to the greatest excitement for very little reason. Such a person seems to have been split up into bits or driven out of sight by the tribulations of life.

Multiple Personality

There have been a very few well-documented cases of multiple personality. These cases differ from a psychosis in two important ways. An individual with multiple personality does not shift with bewildering frequency from one attitude to another but remains a more or less stable personality for long periods before the personality completely changes. In other words, each personality that takes control is more or less adequate to the demands of life but now and again hands over control to one of the other personalities. In the two best-known cases only two personalities were originally involved, although a third appeared after treatment had started.

In the more recent case ('Evelyn Lancaster') the two original personalities were known as 'Eve White' and 'Eve Black'. Eve White knew nothing of the other, but Eve Black claimed to know anything she wanted to know about Eve White (though there was much that she did not bother about!). Eve Black was the personality which disturbed the normal life of Eve White, and on at least two occasions when she got herself into situations that she could not control she simply 'disappeared' and left Eve White to take control.

The Ego

Simple 'odd things' that we all come across, like dreams and slips of the tongue, neuroses and psychoses, have one thing in common—they all involve behaviour that people do not deliberately plan, that they do not intend and that they are not responsible for in the way in which they are responsible for the normal ordering of their lives. In order to talk about things like this one needs to be able to distinguish between the things that a person does deliberately and intentionally and those that, as it seems, happen through a person. In order to do this we speak of the 'ego' when we are thinking about deliberate and conscious action. In other words, the ego controls the life of a normal person except when 'odd things' occur, and we speak of the ego as 'the centre of consciousness'. It is perhaps more correct to think of the ego as a group of conscious psychic elements that are so bound together that they usually co-operate with each other. When we think of the ego like this we can then think of the odd things as the result of interference with the work of the ego by other psychic elements that we do not know about but that influence our minds.

Simple odd things occur in the life of a person who has a relatively developed ego and they do not cause any very great disturbance in his life. The neurotic person has a relatively weak ego and although it normally keeps control of the person's life it is subjected to great interference by other psychic forces which prevent it from dealing adequately with the problems of living. Psychosis affects the ego itself. The ego may give up the attempt to control life in the real world and retire into a world of dreams, or it may be completely overthrown from time to time by some other force (or forces) which takes control for a greater or longer period. Except when the ego is in control the psychotic person does not seem to be complete at all, but in the rare case of multiple personality the separate sources of control all seem to be reasonably well organised as 'egos' in themselves and that is why each one behaves like a relatively normal person.

The Unconscious

'The unconscious' is the name given to the 'container' of the 'somethings' that are able to interfere with the normal conscious directions of life. Since it is found convenient to talk as though these unknown things in an individual can take control, it is also convenient to picture those things as somehow existing in the individual. We say that they are 'unconscious', or that they are 'in the unconscious'. Thus, for example, if we mean to speak kindly and friendlily to someone and a hard and bitter phrase slips out we may say that we had an unconscious desire to hurt and distress that person, even though we thought we felt entirely amicable towards him.

It is very important and sometimes difficult to remember that if something is unconscious we really do not know anything about it. When, for example, we claim that a slip of the tongue reveals an attitude to someone else that we do not know about we do not expect that we shall then realise that we do take that attitude to them. Even people who are used to using psychological terms sometimes make this mistake and it is very irritating when they do. When, for instance, an unkind phrase slips out one might say to the person who let it slip, 'It looks as though you have an unconscious dislike of that man'; if he replies, 'Not at all, I admire him tremendously and regard him as the most delightful person imaginable' that shows that he has not the least real idea of what it means to say that something is unconscious. The difficulty is that there are degrees of unconsciousness and there are times when an odd thing does bring home to us the existence of an attitude or idea that we did not realise we had before; this may happen, but there is no reason why it should, and when we think that we can see how an odd thing reveals some unconscious attitude or idea we do not expect the person concerned to know any more about it than we, who are watching him, can see.

The unconscious is only known by the way in which it influences a person's life and when we talk about the unconscious we are talking about the odd things to which we have referred above—the things that do not 'fit' into what we know of ourselves. It is not really correct to say that there are things 'in the unconscious' because, if there are, we can never know them, nor examine them as we can examine the brain or an amoeba under the microscope. What we have really done is to form a picture in our minds that helps us to talk about odd things. In fact, it is found that this picture is extremely helpful in a great many ways, and this is the reason why we are justified in using it.

Even if we construct a situation in which it looks obvious that things were at one time unconscious and then became conscious, we could not say that if it actually took place we should have proved that the unconscious exists. Suppose, for example, the following:

1. John has met and made love with a number of girls, but apart from sex he has little interest in them. He gets to know Janet who fascinates him, although she is not what he thinks of as 'his type'. He finds he can talk to her easily about interesting things. After a time he tries to make love with her, but finds he is unable to.

2. John is confused about several things. He cannot understand why Janet fascinates him; he is surprised at the way they talk together and he is shocked at his impotence. He seeks help and eventually comes to believe a story about the unconscious. Janet has certain features that, although he had not noticed it, remind him of his mother. The way they talk together is very like the way he used to be able to talk with his mother in his late teens. Although he had never known about it he had strong sexual feelings towards his mother, and he had got Janet and his mother so mixed up (somewhere 'in his unconscious!') that when he tried to make love to

Janet he was, without knowing it, inhibited by the incest taboo.

3. After some time John's relation with Janet changes. He realises that she recalls his mother in some ways, but although she no longer fascinates him as she did before he finds that he likes her for many other reasons. He recognises that his talk with her is very like his talk with his mother in the past, but now it develops in other ways as well. He knows that he has sexual feelings about his mother and is able, to some extent, to distinguish them from his feelings about Janet. He finds that he is able to make love with Janet.

We can represent these three situations like this:

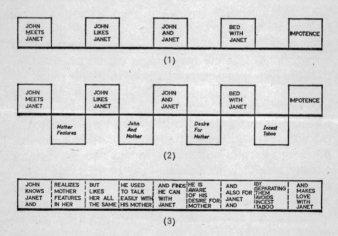

(1)

(2)

(3)

It looks as though what was below the line in 2 has come up above the line in 3, and this corresponds to our habit of talking about 'things becoming conscious'. Even so, we do not know that anything of the sort has happened. All we know is that the situation represented in 1 has developed into that represented in 3. Telling the story represented in 2 may have had something to do with it, but that is as much as we can say.

It is a fact that things happen in our lives that we cannot attribute to outside influence but do not feel responsible for, in the sense of having decided, intended or chosen to do them, and this is just as much a fact about human nature as the fact that we sometimes know just how and why we came to do something. Any full account of human living must take this into account and the idea of the unconscious is found to be a most helpful and valuable way of doing so.

The Psyche

So far we have been using the expression 'the mind' in a very loose way: we should keep the word 'mind' to refer to our mental selves as we know ourselves by introspection. In other words, 'mind' means consciousness. As we have just said, this is all that we actually know about ourselves and the unconscious is simply a picture that helps us to talk about the odd things that happen in our lives. It is very natural that in forming our picture of the unconscious we should picture it as more of the same sort of things that go to make up our 'minds' and imagine a totality that is made up of consciousness and the unconscious. When we do this we use the word 'psyche' to refer to the whole lot. Thus the psyche is the idea of a total inner world which is made up of both conscious and unconscious elements.

Although we cannot know for certain that the unconscious part of the psyche (or 'the unconscious psyche') is the same sort of thing as the conscious part (the mind) we do know that it has the same sort of effect on our behaviour as the conscious part. If we hate someone we are likely to say something nasty to him and if we hate someone unconsciously we may say something nasty by accident: the difference is that we know what we are doing in the first instance, we do not in the second. The fact that consciousness and the unconscious do influence us in very much the same ways is a good reason for thinking of them as two parts of one thing—the thing we call 'the psyche'.

The psyche is a living organism constantly developing, and this is equally true of each of its two parts—consciousness and the unconscious. We can take note of the changes that go on in consciousness and say, for instance, 'I wouldn't have said that a few years ago', or 'I should never have behaved like that last year', or 'My ideas have developed a lot since then'; if we keep a diary, or a very close watch on our thoughts, we can look back and see how our minds have changed and developed over a period of time. We think of the unconscious as changing and developing in much the same way, except that we have no means of observing the actual process of change; what happens is that the odd things that result from the interference of our lives by unconscious elements take different forms from time to time, indicating that the unconscious itself has changed.

4 How the Psyche Functions

A Picture of the Psyche

We do not know what the unconscious is like, so that any picture that we make of the psyche is only a convenient way of thinking about it. That means that no picture is the one, correct picture, and the picture we describe here is only one of many ways of thinking about the psyche.

One is to imagine a cylinder full of water dropping down like a shaft out of sight. A very small section at the top of the cylinder is illuminated and one can see clearly the things that float in it. As one looks deeper, so one's vision becomes less clear and the greater part of the contents of the cylinder are completely invisible. There is considerable movement in the part that is illuminated and one can see how some things slowly sink out of sight, while others rise up out of the depths.

The top, lighted section represents the conscious mind and the things that can be seen in it represent all those thoughts, ideas, desires and so on that we know about. These things are seen to form a kind of pattern: a larger number of them are grouped together to form a fairly dense mass. This mass represents 'ego-consciousness', the dominant ideas and characteristics of one's personality. Other things are loosely connected with this central mass and others have hardly any con-

nection with it at all. It is those things least connected
with the central mass that tend to sink out of sight. The
deep part of the cylinder in which we can see nothing
represents the unconscious.

The Threshold of Consciousness

The picture includes a kind of half-way area between
the full light of consciousness and the unconscious. This
is the area in which vision is becoming obscured, but
things can still be seen as moving shapes. In actual
living this represents the fact that there are many things
'at the back of our minds' that we can easily become
aware of if we turn our attention to them but that we
more often ignore.

We speak of the 'threshold of consciousness' to indicate this area in between consciousness and the unconscious: those things that are 'above the threshold'
are fully conscious and play their part in our lives
almost continually; those that are 'below the threshold'
are unconscious and can only influence our lives in
devious ways. The things below the threshold are said
to be 'subliminal', which simply means 'below the
threshold'.

Examples of subliminal things can be given fairly
easily. At any moment we receive sense-impressions
from our external environment, but there is a great deal
to which we do not turn our attention. We may, for
instance, not notice where the chairs in a room are until
we come to sit down—and then we find that we know
where to sit; we may remember some feature of a room
after we have left it, even though we do not remember
noticing that feature when we were in the room; we
may have forgotten the look of a street that we once

knew very well and yet recall it in detail if we happen to return to it; we may have bits of knowledge 'tucked away' in the back of our minds that we are not called upon to use but we can 'bring out' unexpectedly if occasion should arise. These subliminal things are not normally 'there' in consciousness, but they are in no way lost and can be 'fished up' if they are wanted.

Things that are subliminal in this way pass in and out of consciousness, that is they are able to move across the threshold of consciousness. This is fairly easy to understand. It is not quite so easy to understand how the threshold of consciousness can move. In the picture this simply means that sometimes the lighted area of the top section becomes larger and at other times smaller, but it can also mean that the light can move away from the main group that represents the ego-centre of consciousness to some other part of the cylinder. The enlarging and decreasing of the lighted area is connected with 'concentration': to concentrate is to direct our attention to one or two specially selected ideas or images in our minds and to ignore all the rest. This means that very much more is subliminal than is usually the case and we can express this by saying that the threshold of consciousness has been raised. For instance, if one is studying very hard the noise of a bell which one would normally notice may not 'get through' at all and one may not know that it has rung. On the other hand, when one's mind is relaxed or drifting the threshold of consciousness is lowered and thoughts and images may come into it (out of the unconscious) that one had not been aware of before. The shifting of the light from the central part of consciousness represents the experience that sometimes accompanies an overpowering emotion such as fear or love. At such times the normal attitudes, principles and habits may be completely forgotten and one is guided by powers from within which would normally be controlled. This is, in effect, a lowering of the threshold, whereby unconscious elements are able to play a greater part than usual in one's life.

The Unconscious

As we have said, the dark, lower part of the cylinder represents the unconscious, and there are one or two things that must be remembered about it. It is dark, which means that we do not know what is in it, but at the same time the things in the unconscious are able to affect consciousness. They do this in two main ways. First of all, they cause us to have ideas, thoughts, moods and images in our conscious minds, and this is both an advantage and a disadvantage. It is an advantage because we could never develop our conscious minds at all if we did not receive new things from the unconscious. It is a disadvantage because these things sometimes interfere unduly with our conscious thinking and planning. The things in the unconscious can also sometimes take control of the body and influence our physical behaviour—and, in particular, our speech.

So far we have simply thought of the unconscious as a dark lump lying beneath consciousness, but in the course of their work psychotherapists have found it necessary to picture the unconscious as a changing structured arrangement of parts with its own divisions and organisation.

What we have said in this chapter is more or less generally accepted by all psychotherapists, but when one begins to discuss the structure of the unconscious the divisions between the psychotherapeutic schools start to become important. They are mainly divided by the way in which they picture the internal arrangement of the unconscious psyche. In the remainder of this chapter we shall continue to explain certain ideas that are common to all schools.

Repression

There is general agreement that many of the things in the unconscious have become unconscious as a result of repression, and the idea of repression is used in all forms of psychotherapy. This means that there are some things in the unconscious that, at one time or another, have been conscious, and 'repression' is the word used to indicate that this has happened. Repression is very closely connected with forgetting.

Someone once pointed out that the ability to forget is quite as valuable and remarkable as the ability to remember. It is always nice to be able to remember something, but if we were to remember every single thing that had ever happened to us there would simply be no room in our minds at all. We should be smothered by our memories. The process of forgetting is represented in our picture when a thing falls into the darkness, out of the light of consciousness—that is, when it becomes subliminal. We must say that such things are subliminal, not that they have gone out of our minds, because it is a well-known fact that long-forgotten memories can be revived under the influence of the right stimulus: although we may have forgotten something there is an important sense in which it is still 'there' in our psyche and this is what we mean by saying that it is unconscious.

The difference between forgetting and repression is largely a matter of degree and it is marked by the difficulty of bringing something back to consciousness at the appropriate time. Something that has merely been forgotten can usually be recovered if it would be useful, but a thing that has been repressed can only be brought back into consciousness after great effort; much psychological analysis is concerned with the recovery of repressed things. Whereas we may think of forgotten things as things that have sunk gently out of consciousness it is as though repressed things have had a great weight attached to them to ensure that they shall not float up again.

Why should some things be repressed? The answer is that we repress those things that we feel cannot be accepted within the central organisation of consciousness. For example, if there is a dominant desire in consciousness, then we shall tend to repress a principle that lays it down that such a desire should not be fulfilled; if a certain principle is an important feature of consciousness then we shall repress a desire that could only be fulfilled at the expense of that principle. We also repress those things that destroy our idea of what we are. For example, if someone has done a mean and cowardly thing he has to make a choice: either he must admit that he is the sort of person who is liable to do this sort of thing or he must put the fact that he has done it entirely out of mind—that is, he must repress the memory of it. If he admits that he is the sort of person who might do such a thing he cannot go on thinking of himself as a brave man as, we must assume, he did before. The things we repress are things that would endanger our idea of ourselves if we remembered them—either by proving that we are not the sort of person we like to think we are or by tending to lead us to do things that do not fit in with our idea of ourselves. A former Archbishop of Canterbury remarked about sexual sins: 'We must tell our people that they should not do these things, nor desire to do them', and this was a recommendation that people should not merely control but also repress their sexual desires—that is, thrust them out from their conscious minds. Repression is the way in which we evade moral problems: instead of admitting that there is a clash between different aspects of our nature and seeking to cope with it we simply reject one side in favour of the other.

It is usual to speak of repression as though it were something that is always bad, but this is not the whole truth. Although there is usually something undesirable about repression it has its part to play in the development of the individual. The things that are repressed are things which are some kind of threat to the stability of consciousness. For example, one may repress a painful memory of some foolish or irresponsible act, because if one were to remember it one would lose confidence in oneself and be unable to cope with one's work and duties, or one may repress a bad act because remembering it would make it almost impossible for one to develop the better side of one's character. Sometimes repression of things like this is absolutely essential if a person is to grow and mature—although it may become equally essential to remember what had been repressed when growth has progressed sufficiently. Repression plays a specially important part in the early stages of adult life, when the most important thing for the young person to do is to develop an organised and stable ego-consciousness with which to confront other people and the world. Yet when all this has been said it is still true that repression is more undesirable than it is a good thing, and there are two main reasons why.

The first reason why repression is more bad than good is that it means losing some part of oneself. When we wholly forget something we have thought or done, or something that has happened to us it is not merely a matter of forgetting that thing, we also refuse to see that we are the sort of person capable of behaving in the way that we did. If a memory is repressed it is because that memory is in some way bound up with a tendency within us that we prefer to think we do not have, and from this point of view repression means the loss of something that belongs to us and with which the ego must eventually come to terms. To say this, that the ego must come to terms with the repressed aspect of our nature, is to introduce the idea of 'ought' and it is always dangerous to do this in connection with psychology. It may be that there are things that would be so destructive to a man's character if he did not repress them that it is much better that they should remain repressed and it is certain that there are right times for everything, so that it may well be that it is better not to recover a repressed memory at some particular time. If, for example, a person represses a very large number of things and still manages to live a full, useful and satisfactory life it would probably be wrong to say that he ought to come to terms with the things he has repressed. The idea that we 'ought' to become aware of repressed memories comes from the feeling that the development of the whole of our nature is a good thing, and if this is indeed the case it follows that repression is a bad thing, because it makes it impossible for the repressed aspects of our nature to be included in our organised consciousness.

The other reason why repression is liable to be a bad thing is that it does not do what we should like it to do. If we repress the memory of some occasion when we behaved in a thoroughly selfish and unpleasant way we are able to think of ourselves and behave as though we were unselfish and pleasant, but this does not alter the true facts. If we did on some occasion act selfishly this was because there are selfish elements in our characters, and by repressing the memory we have merely refused to admit this—we have not 'got rid' of the selfish elements. In other words, although the result of repression may be that we do not know about a particular tendency within us, that tendency is still there and it is liable to interfere with our conscious aims. This is often very marked in relation to selfishness, for example, in the case of a person who consciously works very hard for other people 'never thinking of herself' and then has a complete breakdown which forces others to start looking after her. Again, there are people who arrange things in such a way that it is obvious to everyone else that they have come well out of it and yet imagine that all they have done was for the most altruistic and high-minded motives imaginable. Repressed tendencies are able to cause all kinds of peculiar distortions in our behaviour, just because we do not know about them. When we realise that we have tendencies of a particular kind we can do something about trying to control them, but so long as they remain unconscious we can exercise no control over them whatsoever.

It should be kept very clearly in mind that we do not repress things in the way we neglect a piece of work that we know we ought to do, for example. Repression is not something that we do, but something that happens to us. If we really try to forget something we are rarely successful; things are repressed without any deliberate and conscious choice on our part. Thus to say that 'we repress' something is not strictly correct; it is rather that something is repressed. As we have said, repression is a psychic means of avoiding conflict between our conscious character and other tendencies within us, and this means that if, by some means, we are able to recall something we have repressed this does not make things easier for us—it usually confronts us with conflicts and problems that we had previously avoided. It is important to remember this when speaking about psychological analysis. It is a great mistake to suppose that this makes things easier—what it does is to make a person more aware of his total character and (potentially) more able to take responsibility for all that he does. The recovery of repressed memories and ideas should stop many things going on that the individual is unable to control, but it also sets him a hard task in coming to terms with the recovered memories and tendencies within him.

Devaluation

Repression is one way of avoiding conflicts, but there are also other ways and they could all be grouped together under the term 'devaluation'. We may avoid an internal conflict by refusing to give full value to this or that element of the conflict. 'Devaluation' of this kind is brought about by repressing the feeling-tone and the psychic energy of an element, so that it is quite possible for people to devalue elements of their characters without repressing the element itself, and this seems to be an important fact. Unfortunately, very little has been said about it in most works on psychology and it has not received the attention it deserves. Much is said about repression, and it is clear that devaluation has a very similar result, but in a different way.

When one represses something one does not know about it at all; if a tendency opposed to one's conscious aims is repressed, then the problem is simply removed. On the other hand, one can get rid of a problem by devaluing the opposing tendency, even though one does not cease to be aware that it is present. This can be instanced in relation to sex. Most people have now learnt how it comes about that a person with strong, puritan views about sex often tends to suspect sexual immorality in others and even to go out of his or her way to find evidence of it. This is a classic example of repression—such a person has such strong views about the badness or wrongness of sex that he cannot admit to having sexual instincts and tendencies, and so they get repressed; since they cannot express themselves in the natural way as sexual desires they interfere with consciousness in a roundabout way by causing excessive concern about the sexual behaviour of others. Someone with equally strong views about immorality may cope with the problem in rather a different way. He may be quite ready to admit that he has sexual instincts and desires that are not entirely confined to a marriage relationship, but he may find that they never cause him any serious problem or difficulty. Such a man has not repressed his sex instincts, since he is aware of them, but he has succeeded in evading the problem they might present him by taking away from them their psychic strength (i.e. psychic energy). We do not devalue in this kind of way by conscious choice any more than we deliberately repress a thing; like repression, it is simply something that happens.

Another instance of devaluation can be given in connection with religious faith. The religious fanatic has clearly repressed his doubts, and many others with 'simple faith' are in the same state. There are those, however, who do not deny that their belief rests upon something less than certain knowledge but who manage to admit to real doubts without letting those doubts become a serious problem. In many ways devaluation appears to be a thoroughly good thing—it serves the main purpose of repression without involving one in the more obvious dangers of repression. At the same time, it seems to imply a serious loss. If one has instincts, or doubts, this is a real and important fact about oneself which must result in a real tension and conflict; if one devalues these things one evades the tension, but one also loses the energy connected with what has been devalued. This devaluation of things in the psyche is something that most people can investigate for themselves in their own lives, and it is clearly a very important feature in the lives of many people.

Rationalisation

When something is repressed it still influences conscious life. Repressed elements are unconscious and they express themselves in the 'odd things' of which we have already spoken. It may appear strange that this can go on happening without a person's becoming aware that his life is being influenced by things that he knows nothing about, but this is certainly what happens and people show the most extraordinary ability to remain unaware of odd things that are obvious to other people. In a sense it is all part of repression, because the effect of repression is to hide things away from conscious knowledge. Two simple ways in which we hide the odd things from ourselves are by further repression and devaluation: by repression we simply put the odd incident out of our minds, and by devaluation we refuse to admit that it has any real importance. For example, suppose that we dislike someone but do not admit to ourselves that we dislike that person (i.e. suppose we repress our dislike of him), and suppose that dislike expresses itself by causing us to forget to post a letter to him. It is very easy to forget that we made this mistake, even after we have found the letter and posted it. This is to conceal the odd thing by further repression. If the odd things are slips of the tongue or strange ideas, it is very easy to tell ourselves that they have no importance or significance whatsoever, and if we do this we conceal them by devaluing them. However, the most usual way of hiding odd things from ourselves is by 'rationalisation', which means telling ourselves that they were not really odd at all.

An elderly woman climbs a fairly steep path with a

group of younger people. She not only wishes to show them that she has no trouble in walking up the path, she is also convinced in her own mind that she is just as capable of getting up as the others and quite sure that she does not need to take more rests than they do. Some way up she stops and turns round to look back. Why has she stopped? It is quite obvious to the on-looker that she has stopped in order to recover her breath before going on with the climb, but if she were to think this herself it would not fit in with her certainty that she could manage as well as everyone else. *She* knows perfectly well that she has stopped in order to admire the view, which is particularly delightful at this spot. This is rationalisation and, like repression and devaluation, it is something that happens to us, not something that we do. The elderly lady did not 'think up' an excuse for stopping, she really did say to herself 'I really must look at the view from this point' and she really did believe that this was the reason why she stopped. For her there was no odd thing, nothing that could suggest to her that she was mistaken in thinking she was as capable of climbing the hill as anyone else.

Another woman had been brought up with some-what excessive ideas about modesty, in particular about being seen naked. As she grew up she had corrected these ideas (as she imagined) and realised that there were certain situations when modesty of this sort was not a good thing. When, however, she and her husband made love with the light on she always found that it caused her some kind of distress—it got in her eyes, or it was too bright, or something like that—so that it had to be turned out. Because she planned to be open and to make love in the light the turning out of the light was an odd thing which did not fit in with her conscious intention, but it did not appear to her to be odd because she always had an explanation for it which had nothing to do with her repressed modesty. Perhaps it should be added that there is nothing specially 'odd' about choosing to make love either with the light on or in the dark; the 'oddness' of which we are speaking arises when one intends one thing and does the other. In most instances of rationalisation the reason we find in order to explain the odd thing that happens is a good one which really does make sense, but whether it is or not it always takes us in. It sometimes takes other people in as well, but at other times it is clear to others that the reason we give is not the right one.

From the point of view of the observer a common mark of rationalisation is the multiplication of different reasons for the same thing. Suppose one notices that someone always crosses the road at a particular point, although it is an inconvenient place to cross. If one asks about this on one occasion and is told that it was in order to post a letter in the pillar box on the other side one accepts the explanation, but if on another day the person says 'let's cross over, it's sunnier over there' and on yet another day 'I just want to cross over to see how the flowers are getting on in Mr. Brown's garden' and later on, 'There's Mrs. Green coming, I don't want to waste time talking to her, let's cross over'—then one begins to think that there is something odd about it and one may remember that if one did not cross at that point one would pass a garden in which there was a large dog which barked at passers-by. Again, someone may give a reason for something and his reason may sound a good one, but then one points out to him that it is not really a good one—immediately he offers a completely different reason for the same thing, and when this is shown to be mistaken he produces yet another reason: and so it goes on.

The reason for this multiplicity of explanations is that when we rationalise we are not able to give the real reason for our act or attitude because it is unconscious, and if we are not giving the real reason it does not really matter what other reason we give—all are as good (or as bad) as each other and we are quite content to try them out one after the other: anything, in fact, is better than discovering the true reason. Rationalisation, of course, is like straightforward deceit when we are at pains to prevent someone else from finding out our real reason, but it differs from this in that it is ourselves who are deceived—though *we* do not deceive anybody, not even ourselves, it is rather that we are deceived. We really think that the reasons we give are the right ones and so we are able to avoid noticing that odd things take place.

Projection

Projection is also a means whereby we hide from ourselves the unconscious cause of odd things. By rationalising odd things we are able to admit that we are responsible for them and also to hide the thing that causes them; by projection we become aware of the unconscious source of odd things but hide the fact that it is in ourselves. For instance, suppose a man who thinks of himself as good-natured and tolerant has a repressed and unconscious hatred for someone else. When a quarrel flares up between them it is an odd thing and

the man may either rationalise it or project his unconscious hatred. If he rationalises it he will admit that
he caused the quarrel but explain it away as the result
of a hard day's work or of some source of irritation not
connected with the other man: that is, he accepts
responsibility while hiding the unconscious cause. If he
projects his hatred he will claim that the other person
started the quarrel and that he did so because of his
dislike of the first man. The man with unconscious
hatred thinks that the hatred comes from the other man.

The prudish person who finds sexual immorality
everywhere is also projecting. He or she denies the
strength of his own tendency to sexual immorality but
makes the assumption that other people (often the
young) are obsessed by their sex instincts—he sees in
others what he refuses to see in himself. A more complicated form of projection occurs when people 'fall in
love' and seem to see the person with whom they are in
love through a kind of shining cloud. What has happened is that an idealised idea of what a woman (or a
man) should be exists in the mind of the young man (or
woman) and he projects this upon the actual woman—
that is, he does not see her as she really is but as an
embodiment of his own ideal. Such a projection makes
it impossible for a man to see what the woman is really
like, and it is very often most irritating to the person on
whom the projection is made. In this instance it is not
so much an unconscious tendency that has been projected as a complicated idea in one's mind of which one
is not fully conscious. When we project we become
aware of things that are in our own unconscious, but we
become aware of them, as it were, in the wrong place.
It is very like a magic lantern which projects an image

whom it is made. First, it should be realised that we rarely project something on to someone else unless there is some reason for doing so. For example, if John Smith has an unconscious hatred for Peter Brown he is not likely to project that hatred (that is, to think that Peter Brown hates him) if Peter Brown is absolutely free of all (conscious or unconscious) dislike of him. The act of projecting tends to arouse the dormant dislike in Peter Brown, so that, as a result of the projection, Peter Brown does actually behave in a more unpleasant way towards John Smith than he would otherwise have done. Again, if one has repressed one's more severe and 'schoolmistressy' attitudes and projects them on to someone else, then that other person probably will speak to one in a schoolmistressy way. These effects of projection are obviously of great importance in personal relationships and a lot of misunderstandings can be avoided by those who are aware of the power that projection can have in constellating in the other person characteristics that would play a very minor rôle if it were not for projection. For example, if one has treated someone unjustly but refuses to admit it, then projects upon him a sense of being badly treated he may act accordingly, but if one can bring oneself to admit the truth there is no projection and the person who has been badly treated is likely to behave in a much more understanding way (if he is an understanding person to begin with!).

Complexes

Psychic elements do not exist in isolation, either in consciousness or in the unconscious. For example, we do not often have a single, simple attitude to another person: we find this person admirable but dull, another person fascinating and at the same time someone we disapprove of, and so on. We may take a complex attitude to our job: it may be to us a necessary nuisance, an interesting job, hard work and an escape from tensions at home—and it may be all these things at the same time. 'Being in love', friendship, rivalry and many other common relationships between people are extremely complicated, and they are made up of a number of elements which are bound together to form a whole. This tendency for psychic elements to become bound together accounts for the fact, for instance, that we find it difficult to disapprove of someone we like very much or to like someone of whom we disapprove—even though the person we like may do things of which we would normally disapprove and the person we disapprove of may be very likeable.

Consciousness itself is really a large complex and our conscious character is formed from an immense number of elements, many of them grouped together in subsidiary complexes. The more stable a person is, the more closely bound together are the elements that form his consciousness, and the less united they are, the more likely he is to behave in inconsistent ways. There are many people whose conscious character seems to consist of one or two complexes that have little relationship to each other: such people may be said to be 'one person at work and another in his own home', or it may be said 'he is a different person again when he gets with a group of his special cronies'. On the whole, there is something that strikes us as 'reasonable' in the grouping of elements in consciousness and complexes are usually formed for sound reasons, but even in consciousness it often happens that complexes tend to cause errors of judgement. For example, if someone has been extremely badly treated by a person with a beard he may connect the idea of an untrustworthy person with the idea of a beard and he may tend to suspect people with beards. Normally this will be no more than a tendency and it will soon be corrected in particular cases, but certain complexes of this sort cause widespread chaos—for example, the complex connected with Jews in Christian Europe (rooted in the condemnation of the Jews for crucifying Jesus) or the complex attitude of white-skinned races to black-skinned people, which is connected with the contrast between light and darkness.

If conscious complexes are sometimes less than reasonable it need cause no surprise that complexes in the unconscious should be largely unreasonable. It seems that psychic elements tend to become connected together, and if they are unconscious they may be bound together for reasons that seem to be wholly trivial. Unconscious connections between psychic elements may depend upon similarity of sound or appearance, the fact that two things occurred at the same time, a pun and so on. What happens when elements are grouped together like this is that the attitude and energy belonging to one is shared with the other, and so long as the whole thing is unconscious we can do very little to overcome this. If, for example, one has repressed the fact that a man with a beard has let one down badly, then one will have no way of discovering why it is that one never manages to get on with people who wear beards and the expectation that people with certain names will behave in appropriate ways is largely due to unconscious complexes formed from our previous experience of people with those names (both in real life, in literature and at the cinema).

The tendency for unconscious elements to form into complexes means that when something is repressed it gets attached to things already in the unconscious and this influences both the repressed element and the thing to which it becomes attached. For example, suppose a fairly trivial misdemeanour is repressed, it may well become bound up in the unconscious with far more serious tendencies to evil and so influence us (through 'odd things') far more devastatingly than it would have done otherwise. Again, if we repress something as evil it may get connected with something rising out of the unconscious which should become conscious, and if it does it will tend to act as a 'sinker' which prevents that thing from becoming conscious. For example, someone who has had an unhappy and unfortunate love affair may repress the worst features of it, and they may then become bound up with a later tendency to fall in love with someone else and make this impossible. There will be more to be said about complexes in later chapters.

Summary

The main psychic activities explained in this chapter are:

Repression—the complete failure to recollect certain past events and the complete ignorance of the existence of certain aspects of our character.

Devaluation—the effective neutralisation of some aspect of our character by removing psychic energy from it.

Rationalisation—the conviction that one knows why one did something when, in fact, the reason was quite different.

Projection—attributing our own unconscious tendencies to other people.

It is necessary to remember that all these things are things that happen, not things that we choose to do. We cannot purposely repress a thing because we have to know about it to do this, and if we know about it, it is not repressed. If a thing is repressed we simply do not know it. In order to purposely devalue something we should have to be aware of its strength, but if it is devalued we simply do not realise it is an important tendency within us. When we project we have no idea that we are doing so and think that the other person is responsible for all that is going on. It seems that it must be true that we are in some way 'responsible' for these things, but we are not responsible for them in the way we are responsible for our conscious choice and decisions—these things simply happen, and the most that can be said is that when they happen to us they do so because we are the people we are. It is some comfort to remember that they happen to everyone!

5 The Collective Unconscious

Divisions of the Psyche

All psychotherapists think of the psyche as having the two parts of which we have spoken—consciousness and the unconscious, and there cannot be any very serious differences of opinion about what is found in consciousness, because this is known to anyone who practises a little introspection. Different schools of psychotherapy, however, vary a great deal in their approach to the way in which the rest of the psyche is thought of. As we have seen, Freudians think in terms of Id, Sub-conscious, Ego and Superego, and this is one way of dividing the contents of the psyche into groups. In this chapter we shall describe the jungian picture of the psyche, and according to Jung the important groupings of psychic contents are Consciousness, the Personal Unconscious and the Collective Unconscious. This way of dividing the psyche into groups was introduced by Jung and it forms one of the most important distinguishing features of his teaching. The idea of the Personal Unconscious is easier to understand than that of the Collective Unconscious.

The Personal Unconscious

The account given in the last chapter of what might be called the 'top layer' of the unconscious would probably be accepted by the majority of psychotherapists. It is generally agreed that there are in the unconscious things that have, as it were, 'fallen out' of consciousness— memories that we have forgotten, things that we have seen or heard without taking proper notice of them, habits and tendencies of one sort or another. It is also generally agreed that there are things that have been repressed and that these things tend to group together to form unconscious complexes. There might not be quite so much agreement about a further group of things that Jung says are in the top layer of the unconscious. These are things that have never been conscious but are on the way to becoming conscious.

The idea that there are things that start in the depths of the unconscious and slowly work their way up into consciousness may seem, at first sight, to be slightly curious, but it accords very well with our everyday experience. Anyone who has had anything to do with the personal development of another person (whether he be a psychotherapist, priest or university tutor, for example) soon realises that it is not enough to tell that person something; he must be ready to receive and accept it before it can mean anything to him at all. It is a common (and yet always surprising) experience to have repeatedly pointed something out to a person over a period of weeks, months or years and then to hear him suddenly saying exactly the same thing in a tone of great surprise, as a new truth which he has just discovered. The same thing, of course, is true of the education of children; a child can only be taught certain things at any given time, and if one tries to teach him things that he is not ready to learn he just does not receive them—and it is very unfortunate when a child is not taught the things that he is ready to learn. In other words, 'underneath' our conscious mind there is continual development going on and ideas and attitudes are preparing in the unconscious for long periods before they actually enter into consciousness. According to Jung, such unconscious psychic elements are also in the 'top layer' of the unconscious, and they tend to form complexes with the other elements in that layer. This is why repression can often prevent further development, when something 'on the way up' gets bound up in a complex with something that has been repressed.

It is clear that the things in the top layer of the unconscious are closely connected with the nature of a man's conscious personality. We do not repress everything unpleasant but only those things that are a special danger to us. A man who sets out to keep a very strict moral code is likely to repress the tendencies within him that are liable to conflict with that code; the libertine will repress the moral tendencies that oppose his licentiousness; the man who prides himself on his reasonableness represses his irrational tendencies; the man who aims to be a strong man will repress his weaker characteristics. The repressed elements are repressed because they have some special connection with those elements that are conscious, and the most usual connection is that of standing in opposition to the conscious elements. Thus it can be said that the top layer of the unconscious in any particular person is what it is largely because he is the (conscious) person that he is. In other words, the top layer of the unconscious is bound up with the personal characteristics of an individual and for this reason Jung calls it the 'Personal Unconscious'; its contents and the way they are grouped are different in each individual.

Manifestations of the Collective Unconscious

We have suggested that we can think of psychic elements rising up through the unconscious until they eventually enter consciousness. When we think in this way it is natural that we should ask where they come from, and the answer must be that they come from some deeper level of the unconscious. It is, however, always to be remembered that when we speak in this way about 'levels' within the unconscious we are using a model; we do not know anything about what the unconscious is in itself, and all we can do is to think in terms of models that help us to talk about what actually goes on. We may think of a 'deeper layer' of the unconscious, and we call this deeper layer the 'Collective Unconscious'; but what we are really concerned with are those things happening in our lives that we regard as manifestations of the collective unconscious.

The elements in the collective unconscious manifest themselves in the same way as other unconscious elements, that is by causing ideas, attitudes and behaviour that do not fit in with the normal life of the person concerned; but the manifestations of the collective unconscious are rather different from those of the personal unconscious. Manifestations of the collective unconscious are, in a way, more odd than the effects of other unconscious elements and they often have an outré quality about them. The result of their greater oddness is that there is more resistance to them in the conscious psyche, so that they are less likely to crop up in the course of actual living than are the effects of other unconscious things: they turn up only when one is relaxed and off guard in dreams, or day-dreams, or in special circumstances—and also in serious cases of mental disturbance.

Manifestations of the collective unconscious are liable to be 'larger than life'. It may be odd that an indifferently efficient office boy should dream of becoming the manager of the department, but there is nothing extraordinary about it so long as it remains little more than a dream or reverie. Fantasies about the possible but improbable are common enough and occur in most people's lives. On the other hand, day-dreams that include ideas of having supreme power in the universe and of having the power of life and death in relation to other men and women are rather less normal and verge towards actual insanity. The dream of Joseph described in the Old Testament in which the sun and the moon and the stars bowed down before him has this larger than life quality, and so have dreams or fantasies in which one is seeking for some unthinkable treasure, or some new knowledge which will solve all the problems of the world. Probably such things as these crop up at some time in some way or another in the lives of most people, but most of us are able to detect the fantastic element in them and to refuse to take them seriously. Psychotherapists, on the other hand, encounter instances in which ideas such as these have got such a grip on a person that either he is unable to dismiss them, even when he is aware of their foolishness, or he becomes so obsessed by them that he loses all contact with reality.

Beside the 'larger than life' quality those things that are called manifestations of the collective unconscious are also marked by the fact that they appear to crop up again and again in human history. It is largely due to

Jung that psychotherapists have searched among ancient writings and the systems of ancient religions for parallels to the things they encounter in their consulting rooms. What has been found is that the majority of those dreams and fantasies that have a larger than life quality and strike the patient as being of great importance include ideas and images that are also found in mythology and religion. It is not always possible to prove that there has been no previous knowledge of the older ideas in the mind of the patient, but there are a large number of instances in which it appears very unlikely that there should have been and, on the whole, the evidence suggests that the same ideas crop up spontaneously in different people at different times and places. Among the most important of such ideas are the idea of the hero who faces great dangers in order to reach at last to some treasure, the idea of creation and of absolute evil, the image of the wise companion and guide who leads one through dangers and difficulties, and the image of a great mother of all men.

The elements of the collective unconscious are most easily seen in dreams and fantasies, because these things are least controlled by a conscious sense of the limits of real life, and, as we have said, they are most apparent of all in cases of serious psychoses. They also arise in the consulting room, where a patient may be consciously and deliberately setting aside his critical, conscious faculty. At the same time, there are odd things that occur fairly commonly in everyday life that must also be regarded as manifesting the collective unconscious. For example, a mother or father who has taken his or her parenthood in too strict a fashion and ruled the family with a rod of iron may react to some act of insubordination as though it were blasphemy against God; a man may treat some human preceptor as though he were infallible and able to solve every problem that might be encountered; a Church, a party or an –ism may be thought to offer ultimate salvation, a place of present safety and instructions that can only be disobeyed at one's greatest peril; a woman may appear to her lover to be the most beautiful and wonderful woman who has ever existed. There is always some danger in the manifestations of the collective unconscious, but this does not mean that they never have a proper part to play in a man's life. The examples that have been given are intended to be nothing more than illustrations; no judgement is meant on the value of such manifestations.

The ideas behind those things that are called manifestations of the collective unconscious always have general rather than personal significance: that is, they are connected with things that happen to everyone— things like having a mother, being born, the warmth, light and fructifying power of the sun, and death. When this fact is taken in conjunction with the universal occurrence of the same images and ideas it can be seen why Jung uses the term 'collective', although it is not at all certain that this is the best term. He also speaks of the collective unconscious as the 'objective unconscious' and the 'objective psyche', and he is always at great pains to insist that the collective unconscious is not created during the personal life of particular human beings—in other words, the collective unconscious is not formed as a result of the conscious character of an individual and the individual man cannot hold himself responsible for the character of the collective unconscious that manifests itself in his life.

The Nature of the Human Mind

One can usefully think of the collective unconscious as having the same relationship to the conscious mind as the underlying structure of the human body has to the individual peculiarities of a particular body. The basic structure and character of the human body is the same in all men and the organic processes take place in it according to the same pattern, and yet all bodies are not the same body and some parts of the body vary very much more from one person to another than others. In a rather similar way we can say that the underlying nature of the psyche is the same in all men and women but that each individual psyche is different from every other psyche. Consciousness and the personal unconscious vary very greatly from person to person, whereas the collective unconscious is very little affected by individual variations. This does not mean that the working of the collective unconscious is exactly the same in every individual, without the least variation, but only that there is very much more that is common in its effect upon different individuals than there is in that of other elements in the psyche; deep down the same basic ideas and tendencies are found in each one of us, however we may differ in the more conscious part of our minds.

Jung frequently refers to the deeper part of the psyche as 'objective', and he means a number of things by this. First, he means that it is 'objective' in that it does not depend upon the subjective life of the individual. It is what it is because each individual is a human being, not because he is this or that individual. Secondly, he means that the collective unconscious is

not controlled by the conscious mind of the individual—
it influences our lives according to its own methods,
without conscious direction on our part, very much as
the internal organs of the body like liver and kidneys
carry on with their work without any direction from
consciousness and without the knowledge of consciousness; it is largely for this reason that we have to realise
that we cannot hold ourselves responsible for the ideas
and images that arise as a result of the activity of the
collective unconscious. The third reason why the collective unconscious can be spoken of as 'objective' is
that it is the same for everybody, and from this point of
view it can be compared with the external world in
which our lives are led. As conscious individuals we
have to order our lives within the framework of the
world in which we live, and that world is, in an important way, the same for everybody—two different
people in the same place have to take account of the
same buildings and natural features: in a very similar
way the collective unconscious provides a psychic background or environment against or within which we have
to live our conscious lives and which is largely the same
despite individual differences.

The comparison between the collective unconscious
and the external physical environment leads to further
consideration. It is not only true that the manifestations of the collective unconscious are remarkably consistent, even though they occur in the lives of different
individuals, they can also occur as group phenomena.
Between the two wars of this century, this was very
marked in Germany. It would obviously be a mistake
to suppose that Hitler imposed his own exaggerated and
excessive ideas upon an unwilling mass of Germans; the

fact of the matter was that Hitler gave concrete expression to deep inward urges that were striving for expression in Germany as a whole. This dovetailing of the ideas of the demagogue and the unconscious ideas of the people is the secret of all demagogy, and it is one of the things that gives the impression that the same unconscious elements can influence each individual of a group. It is almost as though the individuals are rooted in one psychic substructure which expresses itself through them, and Jung has compared the collective unconscious to a mountain range, of which individual conscious minds are peaks. This idea of *one*, universal collective unconscious can be very useful for talking about many kinds of phenomena that involve more than one person, but we know so little about the ways in which either conscious minds or unconscious psyches can and do act upon one another that it is always possible that mass phenomena may eventually be explained in terms of communication at a deep level of the psyche.

Indentification

It must always be remembered that the collective unconscious has always been and ought to be unconscious. It may be that in the course of human development things that were once in the collective unconscious gradually become part of consciousness, but this is a long and complex process and over a short period of time there is no question of bringing elements of the collective unconscious into consciousness. The personal unconscious contains psychic elements that should be included in consciousness, but the collective unconscious is the unconscious background that gives

depth and force to consciousness. The collective unconscious plays its part in our lives, but it is part of its
rôle to be an unseen influence in the background, and if
the elements of the collective unconscious do become
conscious they are too 'big' for consciousness to cope
with them.

One could illustrate this by a simple example built
round the idea of the 'Great Mother'. This idea gathers
to itself a large number of elements from human experience, in particular the experience of human mother-
hood on the one hand and our dependence upon the
earth for life and sustenance on the other: we all know
such expressions as 'mother earth' and 'mother nature'.
The myth of Persephone brings out another aspect of
this idea, for Persephone was engulfed in a ravine which
opened in the surface of the earth and this is the idea of
the dangerous, devouring mother. Such ideas as these
can obviously reach alarming proportions, because they
involve the idea of absolute dependence, culminating in
complete incorporation within the mother, and this
goes far beyond the reality of our everyday living. So
long as such an idea remains one among many in the
collective unconscious it is checked and balanced by
others, but if it comes into consciousness as an actual
attitude it distorts a man's life in most undesirable ways.
A man can really and truly become 'engulfed' in something that he treats as the manifestation of the mother-
image. That something may be his own mother, and
there are grown men who are entirely absorbed in their
own personal mother; or the engulfment may take the
form of complete submission to one's physical environment, so that one loses all power of decision and
direction of life; or it may lead to a retreat from all the

paraphernalia of urban civilisation and the attempt to live a life 'close to nature'; or it may take the form of absolute dependence upon a human mother-substitute, possibly a wife.

There is a certain difficulty about the meaning of 'conscious' and 'consciousness' which needs to be pointed out here. There are occasions when one can become conscious of elements of the collective unconscious and gain tremendous benefit from it, but that does not mean that those elements become part of consciousness. It is highly probable that great artistic work, great scientific discoveries and many other similar things result from the fact that elements of the collective unconscious press forward through consciousness, and in analytical experience people may be faced with the tremendous power of the contents of the collective unconscious. Danger arises if the ego becomes confused, is unable to realise that these elements 'belong' to the unconscious and attempts to take charge of them as though they could become an integral part of the conscious personality: it is then that they prove too big for the ego and can cause violent disturbance in a man's life. Great development results from the encounter between consciousness and the collective unconscious if the ego can cope with the situation; if it cannot it is overwhelmed, either being destroyed or identifying itself with the unconscious elements.

If an element of the collective unconscious erupts into consciousness it has attracted to itself a great deal of psychic energy and it confronts the ego with a frightening situation. A relatively weak ego-consciousness is likely to be overthrown, to lose all controlling power in a man's life so that the man ceases to be an organised person at all. This leads to psychosis. A somewhat stronger ego may maintain itself to some extent and try to cope with the unconscious element by 'identification'. This has even more devastating effects than the overthrow of the ego, because the individual who identifies with an unconscious element becomes the channel by which that element exerts influence upon others. To 'identify' means to assume that the unconscious idea belongs to consciousness and that the ego has taken control of it. A man thinks that he has controlled the unconscious element whereas, in fact, the unconscious element has taken control of him. When this happens a man becomes 'inhuman' in quite obvious ways.

A very common form of identification is identification with the idea of the office that one holds. This is a professional danger of clergy and psychotherapists, among others. Both these professions require that a man should stand in the relation of intimate guide to others, and in doing this it is only too easy for the man to take to himself qualities that belong to the deep, unconscious image of the perfect, divine guide. If such an identification does take place in a man's mind, then he ceases to be able to accept the fact that his advice may, and sometimes should, be disregarded and he expects to be treated as a 'special person'—not, he says, because he is special in himself but because of his special function. Naturally psychotherapists are well aware of this danger and take pains to ensure that they avoid it, and the very nature of the clergyman's work provides many checks that should save him from it, but even so the danger remains. The doting mother often identifies with the image of the great mother in her relations with her son and seems entirely unaware that she has completely engulfed his individuality. There are some truly evil men or women who have identified with deep unconscious elements of evil, and many prophets and reformers have identified with divine elements which should not become part of ego-consciousness. Identification results in the failure to be human in certain areas of one's life and, at the same time, in the inability to treat other people as human—other people, too, are expected to submit to the absolute authority of the unconscious element.

Inflation

'Inflation' is the name given to the effect of identifying with an element of the collective unconscious. One is, as it were, 'blown up' into more than life-size by doing so. Most people who have had experience of psychological analysis have had some experience of the power that an unconscious element can have and are on their guard against inflation of any kind. There is a serious danger that some of them 'overcompensate'—that is, they are so afraid of identifying with an unconscious element that they do not exert the power in the world that they should. One form of inflation that is very likely to occur in the course of analysis is that of thinking one has discovered the ultimate truth about the unconscious and about the working of the human psyche, and this is obviously a mistake; yet Jung has remarked that sometimes workers in psychotherapy have failed to publish important insights for fear that their feeling that they have stumbled upon some valuable truth is nothing more than the effects of inflation. In the course of an analysis inflation may also take the form of thinking that one has developed further than others.

One recognises inflation in someone else by a certain rigidity of thought: upon those topics with which the unconscious element is involved the inflated person will listen to no arguments and no reasons; he *knows* and there is only one side to the question. Combined with this rigidity there is a contempt for lesser people who are unable to see the force of the opinions that the inflated person expresses. This can lead to a withdrawal from human contacts and a complete retirement into oneself. Inwardly inflation is marked by the feeling called 'euphoria'. This is a strong sense of inward well-being which accompanies a feeling of one's own importance. If this becomes a settled attitude it leads to serious trouble, but it is by no means clear that it is always a serious and deplorable matter. Everyone experiences a mild inflation when he learns some new knowledge or makes some discovery: on such occasions one feels terribly happy and one is sure that from now on everything will run smoothly and efficiently. Such a feeling can be quite delightful and is usually perfectly harmless —it quickly passes away, one comes up against new problems and one realises that one still has very much more to learn. The fact is that, so long as one retains some critical faculty and one can enjoy euphoria without thinking that it is either lasting or necessary, one has not completely identified with unconscious elements and inflation has only taken place in part. Full identification destroys all critical faculties.

When a man fails to recognise the transitory nature of inflation and tries to hold on to it as a permanent possession, then it becomes a most serious matter. As we have said, he may retire completely into himself to nurse the unconscious element that gives him such delight, or he may be thrown into a series of successive states of great happiness followed by deep misery. In its extreme form this gives rise to 'manic-depression', a mental disease in which periods of intense excitement are followed by periods of the deepest gloom. In the periods of excitement the individual is possessed by an unconscious element (or complex) and by its virtue everything seems true and possible; in the periods of depression the power of the unconscious element is lost and the world seems to be a grim and unhappy place presenting problems with which the ego cannot possibly cope. The excitement and the gloom are equally false to reality.

The Persona

There is another division of the psyche which is of importance in Jungian psychology and that is the 'persona'. From one point of view this lies at the opposite extreme from the collective unconscious and is closely associated with the ego. Yet one does not consciously create one's persona, and in so far as it is unconsciously formed it may be mentioned in this chapter on the unconscious. In order to illustrate the idea of identification we made use of the example of the man who identifies with the unconscious idea of the office he holds, and such identification leads to inflation by unconscious elements: at the same time, it is obvious that if a man has a part to play in the ordered life of society he must, to some extent, accept the responsibilities that go with that part. If someone goes to an official for information and direction he will not be pleased if he is entirely misled because that official has a twisted sense of humour, and if a person in an official position exercises his sense of humour at the expense of clients he will soon have to find some other work! Similarly, a lazy person must control his laziness if he is going to hold down a job in a factory. We can all see that in relation to our jobs we not only have to take what we are into account, we also have to submit to the nature of the job.

This necessity of fitting ourselves to our job is not confined to our work. We also have to live among other people within certain social groupings and we have to take those other people into account. Moreover, we have some concern about what other people think about us. As a result, we are not only the person that we know ourselves to be inside, we are also the person who presents a certain, more or less consistent, character to others. This does not mean that we are two different people, one inwardly and one outwardly (although some people are), because the character that we choose to present to others depends upon our own inward nature—we accept conventional ways of behaviour, but at the same time we select: we do not accept *every* convention of our own immediate social group but make our individual choice. In other words, we do not encounter the world with our 'naked' ego, but we relate to the world by means of a personality that expresses our ego and is in some way suited to the world with which we have to do. Jung calls this means of relating to the external world 'the persona'.

The word 'persona' is a Greek word which originally meant the masks worn by Greek actors, and in one sense one's persona is the mask one puts on when one faces the world. Yet the persona is not a deception, it is what we really are in relation to the world. It is in some way like the clothes we wear in our daily life—they both cover our nakedness and reveal our nature.

6 Psychological Types

The Importance of Consciousness

It sometimes seems as though psychotherapists are more concerned with the unconscious psyche than with consciousness and as though their work is entirely a matter of finding out more and more about the depths of the psyche. If one thinks this one is making a very great mistake. It does seem to be true that we cannot go very far in self-knowledge without having to come to terms with some such idea as that of the unconscious, but we only come to realise this by starting with an exploration of consciousness. A psychology that makes use of the idea of the unconscious makes use of it as a something *more*: when we speak of the unconscious ideas and intentions of an individual we are speaking of ideas and intentions that must be taken into account but are supplementary to those ideas and intentions of which the man is aware himself. No serious psychotherapist would make the mistake of thinking that conscious ideas and intentions are not important; he only wishes people to realise that there are other things that are equally important. Some people have expressed surprise that in his book *Mysterium Conjunctio* Jung stresses the importance of the ego, but this is only a matter of making explicit something that has always been implicit.

Even when one is talking explicitly about the uncon-

scious one is not evading the importance of consciousness, because the unconscious is only known by its
effects, and that means by things that occur in consciousness. Moreover, one is interested in the things
that manifest the unconscious because they stand in
some relation to conscious life. It may be that they are
'odd things', of the kind described earlier, which interfere with our conscious plans and purposes, and it is
this ability to interfere with consciousness that makes
them and the idea of the unconscious important.
Or unconscious elements may overthrow consciousness
and then talk about the unconscious is important because a fuller knowledge of what has happened may be
of value in restoring a conscious centre to the individual.
Again, ideas and attitudes rising out of the unconscious
may prove to be very valuable additions to consciousness, and talk about the unconscious helps us to understand more clearly what is happening and why such
things are valuable.

When one is confronted with another person, whether
one happens to be a psychotherapist or not, one very
naturally asks 'what sort of person is this?', and when
one asks this question one's first concern is with that
person's dominant attitude and approach to people and
things—that is, one is concerned with his 'ego-complex',
his conscious approach to life. In order to help oneself
in forming an answer to this question one has to have
some categories in mind, some way of classifying people;
in other words, one has to have some idea of what
different 'types' of people there are. This does not mean
that each individual can be neatly pigeon-holed, it is
only that if one has some general types in mind one
begins to get a clearer picture of an individual. No one

can be exactly classified and no two people can be put together in one clearly labelled compartment. Jung faced this problem of types very many years ago and his examination of types of people was largely the result of his personal experience. At the beginning of his attempt he undoubtedly had the divergence of his views from those of Freud very much in mind and he felt that this was closely connected with a fundamental difference of 'type'.

The Meaning of 'Type'

Jung has suggested that we should divide people into types in two ways which complement one another—somewhat as we might distinguish fruits both by their colour and by their hardness or softness. A fruit is red, yellow, orange and so on, and also hard or soft, and a fruit of any colour can be either hard or soft. Jung claims that people may usually use one or another *Function* and that they may also take one of two different *Attitudes* to the people and things they meet. The *Functions* are Thinking, Feeling, Sensation and Intuition and the *Attitudes* are Introversion and Extraversion, and each of the four functions may be introverted or extraverted.

A function is a way of coping with and evaluating the things one encounters. For example, several people may look at a stretch of country. One is impressed by the view itself; he is aware of the shapes of colour and the way that the shades of green merge into one another. Another thinks of it in terms of profitable farming. A third recalls the history of England and the different races that have lived in that part of the country and the different social systems that have organised their lives. The fourth thinks how much he would like to settle in a countryside such as the one he looks at. Each of the four values the view in a different way and the same view means something different to each one of them. Again, one man sets out to establish himself in the world and his job by the efficiency and ruthlessness of his thought; another relies upon his ability to 'understand' people and to treat them in the way that will incline them towards his cause. One man plans every interview and conversation in detail beforehand, another leaves an interview to form itself as it goes on. One person allows for the irrational in other people, another expects them to accept what he says if he can show that it is reasonable.

The different functions are all at the disposal of every individual, but for one reason or another we develop one and ignore another. Even so, this does not mean that we never use a function that we usually ignore and we may find that it comes into play without any intention on our part, either constituting a valuable addition to what we are at or causing considerable confusion. It is not that some people have one function and not another, but that each one of us is more inclined to use one rather than another. When one distinguishes people according to their dominant function one is simply referring to the way in which they most usually behave.

The dominant function is concerned with the way that people deal with the things that interest them and with what aspect of those things they think important. The other distinction, that between introversion and extraversion, is concerned with people's relationship with the things that interest them. Suppose two people are looking at the same picture. The first person admires the picture for the arrangement and balance of the colours, the technical mastery of the artist and so on: for him it is the picture that is admirable for what it is in itself. The more he looks at the picture, the more he becomes aware of its character and of the effort that went into making it. The other person also admires the picture, but he admires it because of what it does to him: as he looks at the picture he is aware of new insights, new attitudes to life, new ranges of feeling, and the more he looks at the picture, the less he is aware of what the picture is in itself and the more he is aware of the inward response it evokes. Both ways of looking at the picture have dangers when they are carried to an extreme: the first man comes to see in the picture many things that are not really there—that is, that are there for him but not for other people. This happens because he is completely unaware of his own reaction to the picture. The second man is liable to ignore the importance of the picture, to become fascinated by what is going on inside him and to suppose that his response is unique.

Every experience is mixed; something about it is due to the thing we experience and something about it is due to what we are in ourselves: we say that it has both an 'objective' and a 'subjective' aspect. The objective aspect is contributed by the 'object'—the person or thing with which we have to do—and the 'subjective' aspect is the contribution we ourselves make to the experience. This means that it is as wrong to suppose that a particular experience is what it is solely because we are what we are as it is to suppose that everyone has the same experience in the same situation. The extravert is one who stresses the importance of the object in relation to the total experience; the introvert is one who stresses the importance of the person who has the experience. Putting it another way, the extravert thinks that the people and things he encounters give value and importance to his life; the introvert thinks that the really important things are connected with the way in which he encounters those things.

Thinking

'Thinking' is rather an unfortunate way of describing one of the main mental functions, because there is a sense in which all that goes on in our minds can be called 'thought'. It is difficult to think of a better name and there is some justification for its use in that it refers to that kind of thought which most people think of as 'real' or 'proper' thought. Thinking is a 'rational' function which compares and relates things and distinguishes them from one another.

When we use this function we tend to divide a combination of things into separate parts. To 'think' about something (in this sense of 'think') is to consider how it is made up and how the parts are related to one another. We are thinking (in this sense) when we think about the way in which one thing causes another or about the likely effects of a certain action; we are thinking when we arrange things in classes according to categories—when we see, for example, that we can divide animals into those that lay eggs and those that bring forth their young alive; we are thinking when we compare one thing with another, seeing that this is bigger than that or that this is more useful than that.

If one listens to a piece of music and notices the way in which it is constructed, the echoes from other well-known works which are included in it and the aim of the composer, one is making use of the function called 'thinking'.

The tests designed to test the 'Intelligence Quotient' of children are almost exclusively concerned with this function, and for several hundred years European society has regarded this function as the most important one there is. There is some justification for this in that it is by using this function that science and technology have advanced to their present high standard, but it is a foolish and unfortunate attitude in that it creates very great difficulties for those who do not find it easy to use this function. Thinking of this sort is only one of the ways in which we use our minds to cope with life, and those who naturally use them in a different way should not feel that there is something inferior about their thought (in the wider sense). The laws of logic are the account of the way in which our thought proceeds when we use this function.

Feeling

'Feeling' is also an unfortunate choice of name, because we usually connect feeling with emotion and this is not what is meant. Jung speaks of feeling as being a 'rational' function, just as thinking is, and by this he seems to mean that it is a function by which we make judgements about things. But whereas thinking judges the way in which things are connected together and compares them with one another, feeling is concerned with their 'value'.

The contrast between thinking and feeling can be seen very easily in relation to the ideas of value and importance. If we are using the thinking function we can only make judgements about the value of a thing by connecting it with something else of which we already know the value. For example, if one is planning to build a bridge one must start by knowing what the bridge is for and how much money is available and what materials can be had: one does not think about these things, one does one's thinking in order to decide upon the best way of building the bridge within the given conditions. Again, by means of thinking one may discover some means of prolonging life, but one can only say that this has value if one already believes that it is of value to prolong life. By means of thinking we may discover how best to achieve certain goals, and in relation to such goals we may be able to value the means that we think out; but we can only do this if we already know the value of the goals. Feeling is the function that judges value directly.

The nature of feeling is best indicated by the words used in connection with it: they are such words as 'nice', 'nasty', 'good', 'bad', 'beautiful', 'ugly'. When one 'appreciates' a piece of music and makes a judgement about its excellence, then one is making a feeling judgement about it and such a judgement is made upon the piece of music as a whole. When we think about the music we see how it fits together; when we use feeling we are aware of what it is like. In general, feeling is concerned with things in their totality, rather than with the relations between their parts.

Sensation

Thinking and feeling are 'rational' functions by means of which we make judgements about things. Sensation is called an 'irrational' function, because it is neither concerned with relations between things nor with their value. Sensation is the function by means of which we become aware of things as they appear. Sensation deals with the shape, colour and arrangement of the things we see, and it is also concerned with facts. When we use this function we are not concerned with good and bad, right or wrong, cause and effect, or any other relationships or comparison between things: we are simply concerned with what the actual state of things is.

Just as thinking and feeling are two different ways of making judgements, so sensation is one of two ways in which one becomes aware of what the situation is. The other is intuition, and one can illustrate the difference by thinking of two people who see an accident. The person who uses his sensation function sees what happens. He notices how one car comes round the corner, how it suddenly slows and the rear wheels begin to skid; he sees the car slew against a lamp-post, which is bent over, and he sees it slam into the back of another car parked by the pavement. When he thinks about what he has seen later on he begins to work out how the accident took place, but so long as he is using his sensation function he only becomes aware of the actual course of events.

Intuition

The other person who watches the accident presumably sees the same things as the first person, but he is aware of something rather different. He 'sees', as it were, what is going on behind the actual course of events, and the potentialities of the situation. He is aware that the car is coming round the corner too fast, that the driver has to slam on his brakes and he expects the car to skid. He is conscious, all the time, of the problem with which the driver is faced and also of the likely consequences of what is happening. It is not that he does not see what happens but that this is of little importance to him; his interest is in the whys and wherefores of what goes on and the future consequences, not with the actual course of events. He is inclined to dismiss the things that are noted by the function of sensation as 'mere facts' or 'mere events'.

The second person is using the function of intuition. This is not the ability to jump to conclusions but the ability to see the inner meaning and significance of what is going on. This does not mean that intuition is always correct any more than we can always see accurately and correctly what happens when we use the function of sensation. The thing is that the intuition function is concerned with a different aspect of what is happening. The artist who puts on his canvas an almost photographic picture of the landscape at which he looks is using his sensation function; the artist who gives to the landscape a characteristic 'atmosphere', and who distorts or varies the actual appearance of that land-scape in order to do so, is using his intuition function—

he is intuiting and trying to represent the inherent significance of the place.

The Four Functions

It can be useful to represent the four functions by the following diagram:

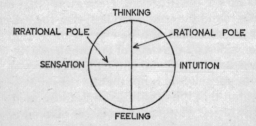

The functions that stand opposite each other are 'opposites', in that they deal with the same kind of thing in different ways. Thus thinking and feeling are both concerned with making judgements, but whereas thinking judges the relations between the parts of a thing and the way in which they are connected together, feeling is the function that values things. One can hardly treat things in both these ways at once any more than one can take a watch to pieces to see how it works at the same time as one uses it in order to tell the time. This means that if one is to develop one's feeling function one cannot pay much attention to thinking and that if one is going to develop thinking one must give little attention to feeling. In a similar way sensation and intuition are both concerned with the nature of things and they can hardly be used at the same time. If one is concerned with the actual appearance of things then it is confusing, in the extreme, if one is also bothered by their significance and meaning, and if significance and meaning are important to one it is only distracting to be asked to consider the exact appearance of things.

The value of the circular arrangement we have used is that it can be said that a person's dominant attitude lies on the circumference of the circle: one may be dominantly a thinking, intuition, feeling or sensation type, or one may be a mixture of thinking and intuition, thinking and sensation, intuition and feeling or sensation and feeling—but one will not be a mixture of thinking and feeling, or sensation and intuition. Everybody has all four functions, but everybody has developed one or two very much more than the others. We can make use of all four, but we each tend to use the one (or two) that we have developed very much more than we use the others, and we also tend to pay more attention to the results of using our dominant function. The person who uses thinking tends to treat the value-judgements of feeling (his own and other people's) as purely objective reactions which are probably rather silly and certainly have no general meaning and importance; the person who most often uses his feeling function thinks that logical thought is dry and arid, a kind of playing with words; the person who uses sensation regards the insights of intuition as a kind of hit-and-miss guesswork; and the person who uses intuition cannot see that there is any value in mere factual knowledge. We speak of a thinking, sensation, feeling or intuition type to mean a person who most commonly uses a particular function and who has developed that function more than others.

Some understanding of these different functions and of the type of person that results from the development of this or that function is very important in personal relations and can prevent many common misunderstandings. Most husbands have been driven half crazy by their failure to understand the value of feeling; when their wives make some remark or suggestion they do not agree with they demand a reason, and they mean a 'thinking' sort of reason. Their wives then try to please by giving the first reason that comes into their heads. The husband patiently points out that this is absurd and the wife tries out another reason—equally absurd. The husband eventually proves beyond doubt that the original remark or suggestion was wrong and the wife reluctantly agrees—later it turns out that the wife was right all along and they can then both see why she was right. Had the husband known about the difference between thinking and feeling he would have realised from the start that his wife might well be right, even though she could give no reason for her claim, and that to ask for a reason was a basic mistake.

The intuition type is also likely to get into trouble when he starts investigating inner causes. One starts with some really horrible bit of behaviour on the part of an individual or a class (the younger generation, for example!) and the intuition type insists on trying to see why and how this kind of behaviour has come about. Very soon he finds that he is being accused of excusing the behaviour and people say, 'but surely you don't think they ought to do that sort of thing!' Of course, he does not think so, but he cannot help being deeply concerned about the underlying motives, and it is important that some people should take them seriously—

although it is equally important that others should concentrate upon the nature of the outward act in itself. In general, we should all be wary of making the mistake of expecting other people to conform to the type that we happen to value and realise that other approaches have values of their own. There is a real danger of persuading people to use a function that they think is likely to be approved instead of that which is appropriate to them.

Introversion

Many people have great difficulty in understanding what it is that Jung means by introversion. Unfortunately, this difficulty besets statistical psychologists almost more than anyone else. The reason why this is unfortunate is that statistical psychologists have concluded that the degree of people's introversion or extraversion can be evaluated by statistical methods, and they frequently devise tests to measure this. As a result, the idea of introversion in the mind of most people is derived from that of statistical psychologists, and this is a very different idea from that which Jung had in mind when he originally introduced the term.

For example, a simple psychological test for measuring degrees of introversion or extraversion includes the following questions: 'Do you butt in on political arguments?' 'Do you get very lively when you are with a group of friends?' The idea is that if you say 'yes' to questions of this sort you are the sort of person who likes taking part in group activities with other people, the sort of person who is happiest in company and who values being among others—and that if you are that sort of person you are extraverted rather than introverted. The extravert, according to this idea, is the sort of person who gets on well with people, enjoys having people round him and does not very much like being alone, and the introvert is the kind of person who is awkward and uncomfortable in a group, and prefers solitude. In popular opinion the distinction is liable to be carried further, and the extravert is thought of as the person who is unselfishly interested in others, whereas the introvert is supposed to be selfishly wrapped up in himself. These ideas have only a very slight connection with the distinction between introvert and extravert as it is made by Jung.

The introvert, according to Jung, is a person who values the inward side of experience more than the outward, but this does not mean that he values himself more than he values other people. As we have seen, Jung insists that there is a part of the psyche that is just as 'objective' as the outer world—that is, it is something that we come into contact with as other than our own conscious self, and it is this inner 'world' with which the introvert is concerned. For example, an idea is part of the inner world, but it is possible to value and work for an idea without being in the least bit selfish: men and women have sacrificed themselves for ideas just as much as they have for other people, or for outward institutions. This concern with ideas is one of the things that shows the mistake made in the kind of questions just referred to. If one tends to butt in on a political argument this may mean that one does not like to be out of a group activity going on around one, but it may also mean that political ideas seem to one so important that one cannot let them be discussed by others without making one's own contribution. Again, if one is lively with one's friends this may mean that one shares interests in common, and one's liveliness may come from the interest one has in the subjects one discusses with them.

The attitude of the introvert is very difficult for people who are not usually introverted to understand. Such people make a very simple distinction between the 'subject' and the 'object', and they describe as 'subjective' everything that is in any way 'inside' themselves and only regard as 'objective' the things in the external world. This is the proper attitude for such people; but from the point of view of the introvert they have identified with their own consciousness many things that do not really belong to it. Because the introvert is concerned with the 'inner world' within himself he is able to distinguish very clearly between his ego-consciousness and other psychic drives and powers, and when he values these things he does not suppose that he is giving value to himself. This can often be seen very clearly in the case of people who are devoted to some party or -ism. If such a person is extraverted he does not distinguish between himself and the idea he serves, and any criticism of or attack upon that idea is taken as a personal attack upon himself; an introverted person, on the other hand, may defend the idea equally strongly, but he will know that he is defending the idea and is not personally involved in the attack that is made. The introverted person stands apart from his inner drives and ideas, and is therefore more conscious of them as entities distinct both from himself and from each other. Thus in solving problems of action and behaviour the introvert finds himself balancing inner drives, principles or motives. The extravert, on the other hand, is more concerned with the opinions of people around and the nature of the different possibilities before him.

Any of the four functions we have discussed can be either introverted or extraverted, but each individual tends to use a particular function in the same way most of the time. For example, if someone has developed his thinking function more than others, he will use it in a predominantly introverted or predominately extraverted way, and we can say that a person who uses his dominant function in an introverted way is an 'introverted' type and a person who uses his dominant function in an extraverted way is an 'extraverted' type. We must remember that, whichever type a person is, he is also able to take the other attitude on some occasions and that, when he uses functions other than his dominant ones, he will almost certainly use them in the opposite way to that in which he normally uses the dominant ones. Thus an extraverted thinking type is liable to use feeling in an introverted way. The differences in types may become clearer if a few remarks are made about the introverted use of each of the four basic functions.

Introverted Thinking

Introverted thinking is most often concerned with ideas, and it is marked by the fact that when one thinks in this way one is only very little concerned with the relation between ideas and external objects. It is the internal arrangement and development of an idea that is important to the introverted thinking type, and if he takes note of the way in which such an idea applies to things it is most often to establish the idea rather than to learn more about the way things work. A person of this sort is always in danger of pressing a scientific theory (for example) far further than the facts justify. The study that is 'a natural' for the introverted thinker is pure mathematics, and the story is told of the pure mathematician in the last century who invented an abstruse calculus: as he put the finishing touches to it he said 'there, at last, is a pure work of art—that no physicist can make use of!'

Introverted Feeling

Feeling is concerned with value, and if feeling is introverted it is concerned with the values of the inner world. Those things that are known by feeling are always hard to communicate to others because our languages are so dominated by the thinking function; feeling judgements about the inner world are doubly hard to communicate because one cannot point directly to the things about which they are made. The result is that the introverted feeling type is liable to be noticed far more for his negative feeling judgements about the external world than for his real and deep positive feeling judgements about the things of the inner world. Such a person can easily form a habit of retiring into an interior world of his own. Nevertheless, he has a very important contribution to make, and if he can feel that another person also values the inner things that seem to him to be of prime importance he can enter into close relationship with that person.

Introverted Sensation

Suppose one is in a church and the sunlight suddenly strikes through a stained-glass window and falls in a pool of red light on the floor. If one's sensation function is extraverted one's attention is drawn to the window through which the light comes, and one notices its colour and design; one may also admire the way the light falls within the church. If, however, one's sensation is introverted, then the pool of red light is liable to call up an inner image, possibly of a pool of blood, and one responds to the appearance of the pool with the sort of shudder that might be appropriate to spilt blood. To the introverted sensation type the inner image takes precedence over the outer configuration. Similarly, with regard to the facts of a situation, introverted sensation records the response one makes rather than the characteristics of the things seen or heard. Much modern art is a deliberate attempt to express externally the features of the inner world revealed by introverted sensation.

Introverted Intuition

Introverted intuition goes beyond and behind the facts about the inner world that introverted sensation reveals. Thus one need not stop at the idea of the pool of blood; one's thought probes further, so that one thinks of the blood of the martyrs and the problems of martyrdom. Or if one is concerned with one's inner response to a situation, then if one uses intuition one sees into the deeper springs of one's attitude—one probes into the pressures and drives that arise from the depths of the psyche and the goals to which they seem to point. It must be remembered that, in doing this, if one is acting in a true introverted way one also distinguishes these pressures and drives from one's own ego: one sees them as truly objective—that is, as things that happen to one, not as things that one is doing.

Extraversion

The extraverted attitude is one that puts stress and importance upon the external object. To an extraverted person true reality is to be found in the world in which he finds himself. His physical environment, his family, the social order around him, the demands that people and things make upon him—these are the things that count, the things that give value to life and the things that he must come to terms with.

We know very many more people from outside than we do from within, because we can only claim to know one person wholly from within. This is probably the main reason why we naturally think of introversion and extraversion in terms of a person's reaction to the external world. What we really notice most is another person's reaction to ourselves, and for that other person we are objects in the external world. From this point of view the introverted person is a person who withdraws from external objects; he holds them (especially us!) at a distance and refuses to become too involved with them. The extraverted person, on the other hand, relates to objects in the world around and is continually coming into as close a relationship with them as he can. Both attitudes are dangerous if carried to an extreme point. At the extreme of introversion a person loses all touch with the world in which he lives; he becomes entirely unrelated to it and becomes lost in a fantasy life of his own. At the extreme of extraversion a person loses his own viewpoint; he becomes engulfed in other people and things and takes on the colour of his environment, whatever it may be.

Extraverted Thinking

When the thinking function is used in an extraverted way ideas are thought of as having value in connection with objects, not in themselves. The introverted thinker will be concerned, for example, with the idea of number in itself, but the extraverted thinker uses number in order to count or arrange objects in the external world. In general, ideas are always *of use* to the extraverted thinker; they are the instruments by means of which he describes, relates and categorises the things he finds outside him. The introverted thinker may look for objects that accord with his ideas, but the extraverted thinker looks for ideas that will be in accord with his experience of objects. The extraverted thinker also pays attention to the thoughts and ideas of those people whom he thinks of as people to be taken seriously, whereas the introverted thinker is interested in people's ideas, without much concern for the status or reputation of the person whose ideas they are.

Extraverted Feeling

We value the people and things that we meet by our feeling function used in an extraverted way. When we do this we do not connect the value we find in the external world with our own inward response (although this may, in fact, affect our judgement) but we regard it as a value that the external object possesses in its own right. A person whose feeling function is extraverted enters very easily into relationships with other people and is liable to accept the 'feeling-tone' of his immediate environment at a particular time without conscious thought or effort. It is probable that in religion introverted feeling leads to a stress upon the inner nature of religious feeling, whereas extraverted feeling leads to a stress upon the symbols and ritual of a cult—that is, the symbols regarded as of special importance by other members of the group.

Extraverted Sensation

It is difficult to see how anyone could survive in the world without using sensation in an extraverted way, at least on some occasions, because it is by this means that we take note of things as they are. By this use of this function we not only become aware of the actual physical arrangement of things in the world around us but we also take note of the state of affairs—the facts of life, in the very widest sense of the phrase. It is obviously essential that one should be able to become aware of things as they are, but if a person is dominated by extraverted sensation there is always the danger that he will become completely engulfed in the march of events and be unable to stand apart from things and relate to them.

Extraverted Intuition

Intuition is also concerned with things as they are, but when this function is extraverted it differs from sensation in that it reveals to one the inner causes of external events and the implications for the future that are contained in them. Sensation concentrates on the behaviour of other people, for example, whereas intuition is concerned with their motives and the likely results of their behaviour. Two general things should be borne in mind. The first is that by means of sensation coupled with thinking one can make judgements about people's motives or the causes underlying events and also about the likely consequences; in this way one comes to opinions about the same things that intuition reveals to one directly. Secondly, one cannot rely upon sensation more than intuition, or vice versa—using our sensation function we may well be mistaken in what we detect as the state of affairs, and using our intuition we may be mistaken about what we understand to be the underlying implications. It is not that one function is more accurate than another but that they are concerned with different aspects of the world.

Unconscious Functions

The functions are all functions of man—in other words, everyone possesses them all in some degree. What happens is that in the course of life one or more is developed as the normal function, by means of which one regulates one's attitude to the world in which one lives and one's behaviour in relation to it. Whether one is more or less extraverted depends upon whether the functions one has developed are extraverted or introverted. Since one also possesses the other functions these are unconscious, and Jung claims that it is generally the case that if the consciously developed functions are extraverted then the unconscious functions are introverted, and that if the conscious functions are introverted the unconscious functions are extraverted.

This means that a man who normally uses his thinking function in an introverted way has, in the unconscious, a tendency to use feeling in an extraverted way, and what that means is that when his conscious mind is relaxed or off guard, or thrown out by some crisis or difficulty, he will behave like an extraverted feeling type. The unconscious function, however, is less developed than conscious functions, so that when the unconscious function becomes active it does so in a confused and even childish way. That is why, for example, an excellent scientist is often remarkably a-logical, and sometimes actually foolish, when he is not dealing with a scientific subject—he often tends to apply to such a subject one of his undeveloped functions.

The introverted thinking type runs the danger of being carried away by extraverted feeling when he is off guard. This might mean, for example, that whereas his thinking was clear, precise and original he tended to accept external judgements of value from those among whom he lived, without submitting them to any serious consideration at all. Again, the extraverted intuition type is open to the danger of being obsessed by inner images and ideas which he becomes aware of through his undeveloped introverted sensation. It sometimes happens that a person who suffers a serious reverse in life gives up his developed conscious function and relies upon a function that was previously undeveloped; this is likely to lead to obsessions and fanaticisms, and probably explains some of the least pleasant phenomena that sometimes occur in connection with religious or political conversion.

Personal Type

It is very useful to have some idea what psychological type one is, but it is not always easy to discover the answer to this question. One reason is that few people rely exclusively upon one function, and also that most people are extraverted at one time and introverted at another. Some people are extreme types, others are not; some rely exclusively on one function, others use two or three. It is often easiest to ask oneself what is one's least used function rather than what function one uses most often. For example, if one has considerable contempt for 'mere facts' and thinks that simply to know what is going on without knowing how or why it is going on is futile and pointless, then one has a very undeveloped sensation function and it is likely that intuition is one of one's more developed functions.

One's own personal type also influences the way in which one describes the different types, and it may be of some help to the reader to indicate the personal evaluations that are involved in the foregoing account. Intuition, whether introverted or extraverted, seems to be an essential and supremely valuable function; and it seems (to the writer, that is—as we have said, our own values are not necessarily right for others) that it is always important to be able to see behind the outward appearance of things, whether they exist in the outer or the inner world. Introverted thinking also seems to be an important function, and to order and relate one's inward ideas seems to be always desirable. Extraverted thinking, on the other hand, seems to be rather dull and silly, and to be bound up with mere facts. Sillier still seems sensation, whether introverted or extraverted, for this seems to do no more than record what is there and to have no special value beyond that—it is necessary, but it cannot take one very far. Feeling seems to be a most valuable function, especially in an introverted form, but it is difficult to understand exactly how it works, or how it can be given a leading position in one's personality. This brief statement is entirely personal and is included to enable the reader to correct for bias in the previous account, although to some extent that correction has already been made. It cannot be said too often that, whatever our own type, *all* the functions have their own value and that it is essential that some people should use each of them as their developed, dominant function. Sensation seems silly to the writer, but to a sensation type intuition will seem equally valueless—not so much silly as unjustified guesswork which may occasionally hit the mark. None of us can ever quite give full value to the functions that we ourselves have not developed.

7 Psychic Development

Readiness to Learn

Every teacher knows that learning must be built up by gentle stages, so that the pupil is ready to take in what he is taught. One must begin every explanation in terms that are already familiar and relate new knowledge to the knowledge that is already possessed. Jung gives a very interesting instance of the way in which the things a person is not yet ready for simply pass that person by. The parents of a young child gave her various items of information about the conception and birth of her baby brother, because these problems were causing her worry and distress: her younger sister was present at the time and seemed to be able to understand what it was all about, even joining in the conversation. In time, however, it became apparent that the younger sister had not taken in the ideas at all and that, as she grew older, it was necessary that she should be given an explanation for herself.

At any given time there are some things that we are ready to understand and some that we are not yet able to comprehend. It also seems that we have limits beyond which we cannot comprehend at all; for instance, it is doubtful if everyone is able to understand the higher reaches of mathematics, however gradually he may be led to them. Probably few people ever reach the absolute limit of the knowledge that they are capable of grasping, but nevertheless the indications are that such limits exist and that they differ with different individuals. It is as though each person has a potential capacity for learning, which he may or may not make full use of, and what is true of learning is true of psychic development generally: the range and intensity of possible experience, reaches of thought, depth of feeling, intuitive understanding and clear vision of the world which are possible to a man vary from person to person, and limits are set in every direction. No one, of course, knows with any assurance what his limits are, nor what are the limits of someone else, but it does appear to be fairly certain that limits of this kind do exist.

The psychic development of an individual can be thought of from two points of view. On the one hand, we can think of the intensive development of a particular aptitude. We all know about this from our knowledge of modern life: one man develops as an expert technologist, another as a specialist in some science, a third as an artist, a fourth as a business manager and so on, and it is a well-known fact that many specialists are very inadequate with regard to subjects outside their speciality. In the terms we have been using this is the development of one or more dominant functions at the expense of other functions and represents the attempt to push the development of that function to its limit. One man may spend a lifetime developing one or two functions, whereas another may reach the limit of possible development very quickly, in relation to his dominant function or functions. The other way of thinking of psychic development is to think of the range of functions developed, rather than the extent to which the development of each one is carried out. This does not mean that all four functions must be developed equally, because it is most likely that the limits of possible development vary between the functions in the same individual; what it does mean is that, as well as developing one's ability in a particular direction, one can also widen the range of one's comprehension and knowledge.

Jung speaks of the opposition between these two ways of developing and uses a rather unfortunate term to refer to the development of one function at the expense of others: he calls this 'striving after perfection', whereas he calls the attempt to bring all the functions into play 'striving after completion'. He uses these terms with special reference to the moral and religious sphere, and speaks of morality and religion as aiming at 'perfection' (i.e. the full development of selected virtues) at the expense of 'completion' (the full use of the totality of one's being). The reason why these terms are a little unfortunate is that in its proper meaning 'perfect' means 'fully formed or made' and it could well be applied to what Jung calls 'completion'.

The Unconscious as Source

Human consciousness today is balanced and complemented by the unconscious. This is how it appears to us from the standpoint of our conscious existence, but in the development of the race (and of the child) psychic life existed before consciousness was developed: in other words, consciousness has developed out of a previous unconscious state. One can picture[1] the unconscious as

---

[1] What follows is a kind of psychological 'myth'; it should not on any account be regarded as a 'scientific account'.

originally containing all possibilities of future development, and containing them in such a way that they 'balance out'. In this unconscious state, we suppose, nothing happens because every element is bound to its opposite and the opposites cancel each other out. This binding of opposites may be indicated by:

The line joining the two circles represents the tie that holds them together and the arrows represent their mutual repulsion. So long as opposites are bound together in this way there is no psychic activity; only if the tie is broken can one of the opposites become effective. If the tie does break one 'rises' into consciousness and the other remains unconscious:

It is easy enough to see something of the way in which this dynamism works in ordinary life. Suppose one has to make some relatively trivial decision—whether to go to the cinema or not, for instance. First one hesitates, then one makes up one's mind and then, immediately one has done so, one becomes aware of all kinds of reasons for not doing what one has decided to do. In small matters this is unimportant and causes little worry, but in large things it may be very serious. When a man is converted to a religious belief, for example, it is never long before the 'opposites' are aroused, and he becomes liable to be beset by all sorts of doubts and difficulties. If he can endure this and accept the values inherent in this 'other side' without letting his faith be destroyed he will be all the stronger, but he is more likely to fear to acknowledge such disturbing thoughts. Such fear means the repression of the unconscious elements and the converted too often shut their minds to the other side in this way, and that is why they are liable to become fanatics—people who shut out all doubts and difficulties because they cannot afford to take note of them.

With these ideas in mind, and using the symbol for the binding of opposites to join complexes of elements as well as single elements, we can represent the original unconscious state something like this:

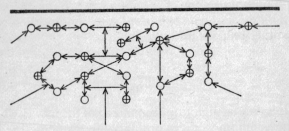

and we should have to understand this kind of thing going on without limit. Why anything should disturb this primordial peace we can have no idea, but if con-

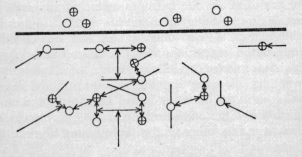

sciousness is to develop from such a state we must suppose that somehow, somewhere the tie joining opposites is broken and elements of one kind or another become conscious. (See second diagram on page 126.)

Synthesis and Disintegration

A man's conscious personality is a synthesis of psychic elements: that is, the elements that make up that personality are related together in such a way that they reinforce one another, and in order for this to be possible some take precedence over others. When the desire for pleasure clashes with duty, the good of others with one's own interest, honesty with the possibility of gain and so on, one does not usually have to decide the problem on each separate occasion. Most people tend to give predominance (i.e. greater value) to the claim of this or that tendency, and to do it consistently. We can rely upon one man to put duty before pleasure, another will continually neglect his duty in the search for pleasure; one is selfish, the other thinks first of others; one man will do anything for money, another is always honest; and so it goes on. This does not mean that there is never a clash, because clashes may occur, for instance, when the usually honest man is offered great gain for a small dishonesty, or when the advantage to himself outweighs an altruistic man's usual concern for others. The tendency to give greater value to particular tendencies and attitudes only means that, for most normal purposes, these tendencies and attitudes seem more important than others. Consciousness is an organised hierarchy of psychic elements, and we may represent the synthesis of psychic elements that have 'got loose' from their opposites and emerged into consciousness by a simple tie, without the arrowheads:

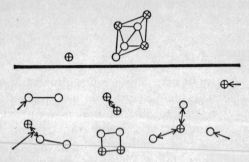

Not all the conscious elements are taken up into the synthesis that one thinks of as 'oneself' (the 'ego-complex'), and as the 'loose' conscious elements group together, so do their opposites in the unconscious. This process continues in the unconscious and one or another complex gathers to itself sufficient energy to 'challenge' the dominant conscious complex, that is it tends to have direct and open influence on the behaviour of the individual:

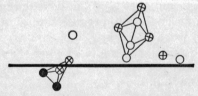

(White and black represent 'good' and 'bad' *from the point of view of the dominant conscious complex.* The unconscious is, of course, still full of elements and groupings not represented.)

The conscious synthesis is what a man thinks of as 'himself', and this means that he has a vested interest in the continuance of the synthesis as it is, so that if the elements rising out of the unconscious present a serious threat to it there is always a tendency for him to resist them.

The tendency to resist any kind of violent change to one's character and personality is natural and important, for if we did not have such a tendency we would be in danger of changing our personalities from day to day, until we were no longer sure who or what we were. At the same time, it carries serious disadvantages, because it means that we are not very ready to receive new psychic elements rising up out of the unconscious. As we have seen, the most active and powerful elements in the unconscious are those that are 'opposite' to the idea in our conscious minds, and this means that they are just those ideas that seem most likely to break up the synthesis which is our egoconsciousness. It seems very much more satisfactory to develop our conscious ideas further than to admit new ideas which seem to contradict them, that is to incorporate further elements from consciousness or the unconscious which are allied and not opposed to those already incorporated in the dominant synthesis. There is a limit beyond which this kind of development cannot go and, sooner or later, the conscious synthesis has to confront the opposing synthesis 'rising' out of the unconscious:

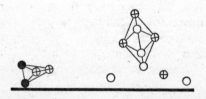

What happens next depends upon the reaction and strength of the conscious synthesis. There are a number of possibilities.

The threat to conscious stability may be so great that the original complex 'closes up' against any possibility of change. It builds a thick shell around itself and thrusts everything else back into the unconscious, that is it represses it:

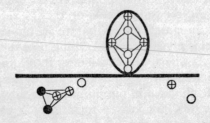

This ensures the dominance and safety of the original conscious personality but leads to a certain inflexibility. It results in a closed mind, for one has established one's character to one's own liking and does not believe that any change would be an improvement. A man who has reacted like this protects his conscious synthesis in every possible way and is unwilling to allow new ideas or attitudes to disturb it. He appears to be a well-balanced, thoroughly consistent individual who 'knows his own mind', but the pain that he (unconsciously) takes to protect his conscious synthesis suggests that it is ultimately unstable and liable to be overthrown if new things should force their way in. His personality and views are fixed, and in some people such a fixing occurs early in life, leaving no possibility of further development.

A second possibility is that the opposing complex may be 'walled off', without being repressed:

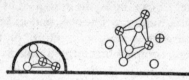

This allows further development of the conscious personality to take place, except in the direction of the ideas and attitudes that make up the walled-off complex, but it means that there is an area of conscious activity where the writ of the dominant complex does not run. In other words, one who has carefully walled off a bit of his conscious self in this way does things that he deplores, knows that he does them and cannot do anything about it. He has a kind of thorn in the psyche. It may be what he thinks of as a besetting sin, or a secret vice, or a black devil which is sometimes roused, or a desperate or despairing mood into which he sometimes falls. Whatever it is, it is something with which his normal consciousness dare not have dealings: it can only be endured, for it cannot be cured so long as the man is unable to face the possibility of a change of character which would allow it an effective place.

Thirdly, the opposing complex may be so strong that it overthrows the original, dominating consciousness and, casting it into the unconscious, takes its place:

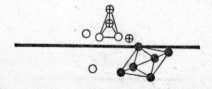

This seems to be what happens in some instances of conversion, when all the old ways are rejected and the old habits change. It can hardly be described as a development since it is, rather, a reversal, and in terms of the present account it is simply a return to the earlier position when a complex first formed itself in consciousness.

Apart from such situations in which the two complexes remain distinct and opposed one to another, there is another possibility. The dominant complex may stand its ground, neither protecting itself from the opposing one nor being overthrown by it:

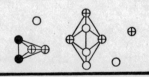

This would mean that one holds on to one's established position, one's ideas and attitudes, and yet acknowledges the existence of other, antagonistic ideas and attitudes which in some way are also one's own. Maintaining, for the time being, one's previous views one realises that they are neither as final nor as permanent as one had supposed. It is obvious that this is not an easy situation to maintain, but if it is held for long enough sooner or later an encounter takes place between the two complexes, causing a disruption of them both:

ing something. In one sense there is no doubt that this is true, but it is true of whatever course one's life follows; if one does not become fixed but develops continually throughout the whole of one's life one misses whatever good there is in getting stuck in a routine early on, and who is to say that one is better than the other? Jung remarks that there are some (fortunate?) people who are never confronted by questions about the meaning of life and their own development, and he adds that if the questions are not asked there is no need to answer them!

The conscious synthesis, which gives a man his character, is liable to be threatened by new ideas, attitudes and images rising out of the unconscious, and the question with which we are concerned is what should be our attitude to them? If one is content to repress them, then one preserves one's conscious synthesis but loses the psychic energy that is bound up in the opposing psychic elements—and there is always the danger that, even though they are repressed, they will acquire sufficient psychic energy to be able to interfere very seriously in our lives. If we are to make use of these new elements—that is, if they are to play a useful part in our lives—we must accept them. This need to accept the elements that oppose consciousness is an important feature of Jung's psychology, and it is also one that it is not easy to understand clearly. Jung certainly does not wish to suggest that we should simply give way to tendencies that seem to us to be bad or evil; on the other hand, he does insist that we should neither pretend that such tendencies do not exist nor treat them as irritating nuisances that we have to control and nothing more. Acceptance of such things means, first of all, that one sees that they are important elements in our total psychic nature and, secondly, that one is ready to let them play some part in one's life. It is important neither to dismiss them nor to suppose that they can be fitted, somehow, into consciousness without any change in one's character.

The real problem is not so much what attitude we should take to the things that oppose our conscious synthesis as what attitude we take to that synthesis itself. If we are utterly and completely content with ourselves as we are, if we do not think that any change in our psychic nature would be an improvement, then we cannot possibly come to terms with those things that threaten our conscious synthesis. If we are to accept these things we must first be ready to change; we must be prepared to allow our personalities to break up in order that they may be reformed in such a way that the new things may be included in a new and fuller synthesis. Suppose, for example, that a man has devoted himself to some scientific work and has formed a habit of giving up pleasure and friendships for the sake of devoting all his attention to his work. If such a man begins to feel drawn to a woman the new attitude will appear to him to endanger his established way of life, and even his character. He thinks of himself as a man wholeheartedly devoted to his work, but he realises that if he is going to take the new thing seriously the woman will be a serious rival to his work, making claims both on his time and on his attention. Moreover, in order to develop his relationship with the woman he will need to make use of aspects of his character quite different from those he has developed in order to carry out his scientific work—that is, of feelings and emotions that he has always despised as things that could only interfere with the way of life he had chosen. All this means that he has to struggle with himself: he must either give up his habitual way of life and admit that there is more to living than the scientific devotion that has always been his ideal, or he must reject the other side of his nature and (probably) the woman as well.

The problem that faces such a man is whether he is able to give up the established synthesis of his conscious mind. If he is, then he can accept the new attitudes and ideas that have been evoked by his attitude to the woman who has come into his life. This does not mean that he must destroy his old character and old way of life, for to do this would be to swing over to 'the other side'. What it means is that, alongside his old ways, he will learn new ways, even though there seems to be a conflict between the old and the new. If he does this, then the new attitudes and ideas will be gradually developed until they are as important to him as the old, and it is at this point that the old synthesis disintegrates in order that a new synthesis may be formed. If this can happen (that is, if the man does not now live two separate lives, sometimes using one aspect of his character and sometimes another) he will achieve a fuller conscious development which includes not only all that made up his previous character but also the new elements of which he had no true awareness before.

Those who go on developing through their lives are continually faced with the formation and disintegration of conscious syntheses. There need be no end to this process, because there is always more in the unconscious that can work up towards consciousness. The formation of such syntheses is not a conscious and deliberate activity; it is something that happens in the course of time as the ideas in consciousness develop. At the same time, we have a certain amount of conscious control in that we can refuse to take note of new ideas coming out of the unconscious. There are many people who are opposed to all talk about psychotherapy and the unconscious just because of this. It sounds as though they are arbitrarily dismissing something that they cannot be bothered to think about, but in reality they are defending their own conscious standpoints against new ideas from the unconscious. They may not be aware of this very clearly, but they do have a sense that the unconscious is dangerous and even evil. It may well be that they are right and that they are not ready to accept new things from the unconscious without destroying themselves completely.

The acceptance of the new things coming from the unconscious is no easy matter. To begin with they are usually things that seem to us to be trivial, foolish or evil, and even to think of accepting them offends our moral sense; secondly, they do not fit with our present picture of ourselves and we do not like to risk destroying it; thirdly, acceptance must not be uncritical. If we bring ourselves to overcome our antagonism to these things we are in danger of giving up our original conscious attitude in order to give ourselves to the new things because these new things tend to fascinate us; this would not be 'development' but simply change. There is also another danger, which is that such acceptance may go no further than adding to our conscious character without creating a new synthesis— that is, we may simply form more habits and take up further attitudes without bringing them into close relationships with those that existed before. True acceptance means giving full weight to the new things without giving up the old and, at the same time, allowing the psyche to readjust itself in its own time and in its own way. It is by no means certain that everyone is capable of doing this, and it may well be that it is best that many people should never attempt it.

The Choice

The kind of development of which we have been speaking is forced upon some people whether they like it or not—as in the illustration of the devoted scientist whose life was disturbed by a woman. Sometimes it is the interference of activated unconscious elements that forces people to do something—although they would prefer to keep to their established ways they are beset by problems that arise because unconscious elements affect their thought and behaviour. This is why it is said that a neurosis may often have a purpose: it may drive a person to do something about himself and so enter on a further development of his psyche that he would not have permitted if he had not been forced to do something about the neurosis.

If one is driven to the further development of one's psyche, one can accept or resist, and acceptance or resistance is mainly a question of one's contentment with one's conscious character—that is, with what one thinks of as 'I'. Development can only take place if one is prepared to allow the 'I' that one knows and loves to be destroyed, in order that a fuller and more developed 'I' may take its place.

8 Archetypes

The Dynamism of the Unconscious

Psychotherapists have been led to study the unconscious because of the occurrence of what I have called 'odd things'. In most people's lives there are occasions when it seems that some perverse imp or devil has got into them and is bent upon making nonsense of all that they are trying to do; there are also occasions when one seems to be guided by some good spirit, a kind of fairy godmother, which sees that one says or does exactly the right thing when, left to oneself, one would have made a terrible mistake. The unconscious is an idea that is used in psychotherapy in order to enable us to deal with things that actually happen in our lives, and because of this the unconscious must be thought of as a source of power. It is not just a box of unwanted psychic elements, it is a continual supply of psychic energy or power.

The personal unconscious, in particular, includes a large number of things that consciousness has rejected. It is obvious that the energy that such things have is not comparable with that of consciousness because, if it were, they would not have been repressed. They achieve power and energy by joining themselves to other psychic elements in the unconscious and forming complexes. The complexes of psychic elements in the unconscious are thought of as being formed round a kind of nucleus, which acts as a binding force to hold the complex together and also provides the complex with the energy it needs to influence psychic life. Jung calls these nuclei 'archetypes', and the archetypes are the main psychic elements in the collective unconscious.

Archetypes are the fundamental source of the energy of the human psyche, and they are closely connected with the idea of instincts. Instincts are mainly concerned with the bodily behaviour of human beings, and when one thinks of the instincts one is thinking of the way in which the human body tends to behave. In thinking of the archetypes one is thinking of the way in which the human mind tends to behave. It has been suggested that the archetypes are the psychic aspect of the instincts, and this may well be true, but so far no exact relationship between the two has been shown. Like instincts, archetypes are basic to human nature and are found in everyone.

Archetypal Images

Since they are in the unconscious, archetypes are unknown to us. We can only talk about the way in which archetypes manifest themselves. It may be that they are best thought of as a way of talking about the tendency of psychic energy to occur in particular forms, because archetypes do not manifest themselves in a 'pure' form. It is not an archetype but the complex that is grouped round an archetype that manifests itself in imaginative images or by interfering with conscious life.

One can form some idea of the way in which archetypal images express archetypes, without expressing them in a pure form, by supposing that a number of authors were all provided with the same basic plot and asked to write a story incorporating it, or that they were each given the outline of a character and asked to write a story about that character. Each story would vary from the others in the details and in the way in which the plot or character was handled, and yet each story would have the same basic theme. It is the same with archetypes. In ancient and modern religions, in myths throughout the ages, in the dreams of modern people and in fiction of all kinds, the same themes occur again and again, but they are always presented in different dress, with individual peculiarities of time and place.

Archetypes and Understanding

The more one is in touch with the archetypes, the more psychic energy is available for coping with the business of living, and that is one reason why those who develop conscious functions at the expense of the unconscious tend to become people of fixed and sterile habits. But this is not the only function of the archetypes. Deep within the human psyche is the deposit of the experience of man since his earliest days, and this deposit sums up the experience of the common and recurring elements in human life. The archetypes represent ways by which man comes to comprehend and come to terms with his external environment. For example, men encounter women as part of the environment in which their lives are lived, and to a man a woman is both like and unlike himself. In order to enter into relationship with women he needs to have some sort of inner aptitude for understanding and coming to terms with them, and it is the function of one of the archetypes to provide him with this.

This function of archetypes reminds one of the simple secret codes one learnt in childhood. One of these involves a piece of paper with little windows cut in it: this paper is laid on top of the paper on which the message is to be written and the message is written in the windows; the cut paper is then taken away and other words are written between the words of the message. In order to decode the message one must have another piece of paper cut like the first, and when one places this over the code message only the true message shows through. In the same way the archetypes provide us with images which we project upon the external world, and

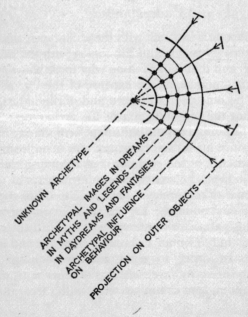

by comparing what we see outwardly with the inward image we come to a clearer awareness of the outer world. The archetypes are not only the source of our psychic power, they are also the source of our comprehension of the world in which we live.

Encounters with Archetypes

Unconscious complexes express themselves to consciousness in dreams and fantasies, and they are also liable to be projected on things in the external world. This means that it is always possible that one may 'meet' an archetype outside oneself. This happens, for example, when archetypes are projected upon a girl, so that she appears to possess a beauty and brightness beyond her actual qualities, when a man appears to be wholly evil without any redeeming features or when a man is accepted as a leader whose judgement is infallible and who must be obeyed without doubt or question. In such instances it is not merely a matter of exaggeration; force and power seem to stream out from the person on whom the archetype is projected, and the person who projects it is unable to use his critical faculty because the archetype exerts such tremendous fascination upon him. Projection of archetypes also gives rise to the sense of holiness attaching to places and things, and by projecting the deepest archetypes in this way human beings stand apart from them and relate to them. Projection of this kind is not something that one chooses to do; like all projection it is something that happens to one, and it has happened throughout human history until the present age. For a number of reasons it seems to happen less in the modern age than it has in the past, and there is reason to think that this is connected with a change taking place in the human psyche.

Our critical faculty is called into play more easily than that of men and women in the past, largely because the scientific spirit of the times has taken the mystery out of the external world. Natural phenomena, which people of earlier ages regarded as the direct activity of God or the gods (for example, the thunder), are now understood scientifically, and our scientific understanding of them prohibits the projection of archetypes. The archetypes, however, do not cease to exist because they are no longer projected to the extent that they were in the past and it is still possible to encounter them; but if they are not encountered in the external world in projected form they must be encountered inwardly. The inward encounter with archetypes results from their manifestation in archetypal images in consciousness, and it is marked by the sense of power and fascination that always goes with the experience of an archetype. One is 'bowled over' by the tremendous force with which one is confronted, one is drawn towards it and one is aware of its quality of 'otherness'—it seems to come out of some other world.

The great difficulty about describing the nature of an encounter with an archetype is that its significance for the individual depends upon that individual's preconceived ideas. The truly religious person will say that it was an encounter with God, or with some aspect of God; the convinced rationalist will either be overwhelmed or succeed in dismissing the experience, probably ascribing it to physical ill-health; 'spiritualists' will ascribe it to guiding spirits and so on. It is only those who use the terms of jungian psychology who regard such an experience as an encounter with an archetype, and it is unfortunate that such people sometimes claim that, in doing this, they are recognising the experience for 'what it really is'. The fact is that such experiences are beyond our comprehension; they do take place and they can have far-reaching influence on the lives of those who take them seriously, but one does not have to talk about archetypes in order to do this. What talk about archetypes does is to enable us to relate such experiences to other things that go on in our lives within the framework provided by jungian psychology —and this is only one of many possible frameworks within which we can attempt to comprehend human living.

The Shadow and the Devil

The archetype that is most easily understood is that of the 'Shadow'. This is the dark, other self that exists in each one of us: it is the dreadful and evil person that we might have been if we had not been so careful to put aside all the tendencies within us of which we do not approve. To a large extent it coincides with the personal unconscious. Since conscious judgement is not always correct we can only say that a man's shadow is made up of what he *thinks* is evil, and in actual fact much that is rejected because a man believes it to be evil is really quite as good as anything in consciousness. Thus it is not true to say that a man's shadow is evil, we can only say that it is made up of things that he thinks are bad. The shadow appears in dreams as a dark man or woman, and in films and television as the bad man who is finally defeated by the hero.

Jung coined the name 'shadow' because this dark side of our character always accompanies us and always seems to us a dark and unwanted part of our psychic nature. He has also pointed out that only three-dimensional things throw a shadow and suggested that if we did not have shadows we should be less than fully human. The archetype of the shadow is formed from the things that we have rejected, and if it remains entirely repressed it exerts a most disturbing influence on our lives; we need to be fully aware of all the 'bad' things we might have been in order that we can subject them to conscious criticism, make use of the psychic energy associated with them and be ready to take responsibility for our own foolishness and bad behaviour. Since the only common fact about the different elements that form the shadow is that they are disliked by our conscious minds we must suppose that there is a deeper archetypal nucleus round which they gather. This nucleus might be described as the archetype of the Devil.

The shadow is a personal matter and each man's shadow is different from that of other men, because each has a different ideal for himself and each rejects different things. Yet there are also evils that are regarded as evil by the great majority of men and there are evil things in the world that we can become aware of if we will. Our understanding of the world in which we live is defective if we are not able to take evil into account and if we are to take the real trends towards evil (both in the world and in human nature) into account then we need some such archetype as that of the devil by means of which to comprehend them. The devil is the eternal opponent of whatever seems to men to be right and good; he represents the principle of evil behind the evil act, the sin that is to be hated even though the sinner is loved, absolute evil unmixed with good. He appears in some form in all religions and in all myths: raised to the status of a god of destruction in Hinduism, relegated to hell in Christianity and engaged in unending conflict with the god of prosperity in the ancient myths. It is around this archetype that the things we repress as evil tend to cluster, and it is from this nucleus that they derive their energy and power.

The Anima and the Animus

The shadow represents the bad self—the man or woman that we might be but do not want to be—and appears as a male figure in the dreams and imagination of men, and as a female figure in the dreams and imagination of women. It may be said, however, that this is only relatively true. In so far as the world has long been dominated by the thought of men the archetypal devil which is common to men and women is usually male, and this is likely to influence the more personal figure of evil in women. As well as the bad self there is in every man a feminine side and in every woman a masculine side, and for a number of reasons there are many people who are not prepared to accept this other side of themselves. They do not repress it so much as 'bad' but rather as 'not proper'. Thus it happens that in the dreams and fantasies of men the shadow is frequently accompanied by the figure of a woman, and Jung has given to this figure (or to the archetype that lies behind it) the name 'Anima'.

The anima, from a personal point of view, is made up

of a man's feminine side and also from ideas derived from his experience of actual women. It is usually represented by a desirable, fascinating and somewhat dangerous female to whom the man is strongly attracted, and the archetype is derived from the fact that, in all his history, man has always been drawn towards women and is never complete in himself. Thus this archetype of the anima has three aspects.

First, the archetype attracts to itself the feminine side of a man's nature, which he tends to ignore. This includes his inferior functions, and by their association with the archetype they acquire psychic power, so that they are able to press upon consciousness. Since this side of a man is personal to the man it ought to be part of his consciousness, and the feminine aspect of his nature can be detached from the underlying archetype and incorporated in his conscious synthesis. This will not make a man effeminate (unless he gives up his proper masculine character in order to accept the other side) but will add to his character components that will enrich and enliven it. Secondly, the archetype enables a man to apprehend and come to terms with the women whom he meets in the world, and it is from this point of view that trouble may be caused by the repression of feminine aspects of a man's character and by his past experience. In so far as the archetype has been included in a complex made up of repressed femininity and by ideas derived from a man's experience of mother, sisters and girl-friends it may tend to distort rather than reveal the nature of actual women with whom he comes into contact. It will have less distorting effect the more successfully a man has detached from the archetype the psychic elements that are personal to him and could be fully incorporated in his conscious life. The third aspect of this archetype is that it holds before us the fact that there is always more. The woman is another who is needed by the man if he is to fulfil himself, and by a natural association the archetype includes the un-finished or limited aspect of all conscious individual life. Consciousness needs the unconscious, the in-dividual needs society, man is dependent, relative and always capable of more, and all these things are in-cluded in the archetype of the anima.

The anima in man tends to appear as an individual woman, but there does not seem to be a corresponding, single image standing for the related archetype in a woman. The tendency is for the dreams and imagina-tion of women to present them with a crowd of male figures, or with a number of relatively individualised men. This is partly a matter of 'compensating' the conscious attitude: women in general tend to give themselves wholeheartedly to one dominating object, whereas men are more inclined to be interested (pos-sibly less deeply) in a number of things, and in the un-conscious the situation is reversed.

Since the anima is usually connected with those functions that a man has not developed there is likely to be an undeveloped or childish attitude about it. This may be apparent in the images that represent it, but it is most apparent when the complex gathered about it is influencing the individual. Naturally this is more apparent to the observer than to the person concerned. When the anima (or animus in a woman) takes charge the individual acts and speaks as though his personality were not his own but that of the archetypal complex, which can be regarded as a partial personality. The anima (in a man) behaves in a wholly silly, emotional and unreasonable way, and some men behave like this when a situation gets beyond control of their reason and common sense. The animus (in a woman) produces a cold reasoning, usually making dogmatic assertions that do not take into account the actual situation in which the woman finds herself.

We are all liable to allow our response to a difficult situation to be directed by an unconscious complex, and in close personal situations in which a man and a woman are involved it is very common for an awkward argument to degenerate into a slanging match between the man's anima and the woman's animus, and this gets neither of them anywhere. It should not be thought, from this, that there is no value in these archetypes. On the contrary, they can provide a means of much-needed understanding between the sexes if they are allowed to play their proper part in life. They also play their part in the formation of personal relationships. A man tends to project the anima-complex upon a woman who attracts him, and it is probably the case that this must be so if a real relationship is to be formed at all. This, however, is liable to make the man see the woman as different from (and usually more wonderful than) what she really is, and if the relationship is to develop the projection must be withdrawn so that a clearer knowledge of the other person can be acquired. A similar process happens the other way round and a woman projects her animus on a man.

The Great Mother and the Magician

The archetype of the Mother represents the origin of the individual; first the actual mother, the origin of the particular life of the particular individual, and ultimately the earth itself from which all life seems to spring. This archetype has two aspects, one benevolent and the other dangerous. In its benevolent aspect it represents the cherishing, nourishing and protective side of mother and earth; in its dangerous aspect it has the characteristics of engulfing and overpowering one— just as one may say that, having been given life by the earth, we are eventually incorporated in it again at death. This engulfing aspect of the mother archetype is often lived out by actual mothers who carry 'cherishing' to such a point that their child has no chance whatever of living a life of his own. The Great Mother archetype includes ideas connected with love—which, like the archetype, has more than one aspect.

The Magician is an archetype that gathers together the male principles that correspond to the female principles gathered up in the archetype of the great mother. The magic wand of the popular conception of the magician is a phallic staff, by means of which he fertilises his surroundings and brings about the beginnings of new life. In Chinese thought these two great archetypes are represented by 'Heaven' and 'Earth', the one initiating, active and fertilising, the other receptive, passive and nourishing. The magician gathers round it ideas connected with absolute truth, and the power of knowledge and even of words. It is the archetype of the power of thought.

Other Archetypes

Archetypes are related to all the deepest workings of the psyche and also to the fundamental and recurring situations in which human beings find themselves. It is impossible to make a list of the archetypes; archetypal images and types of behaviour are marked by the fact that they repeat themselves again and again, and by the fact that they are connected with the presence or release of great psychic energy. The archetypes mentioned above are intended to be representative, but they only illustrate those archetypes that can be personified in imaginative figures. There are also archetypes that are represented by a series of events rather than individual figures, and these are just as important. The best example of such archetypes is the myth of the Dying and Rising God, and this archetype also occurs in the legends of those heroes who rescue a great treasure at the end of a journey through deadly perils.

Gods and Demons

The archetypes themselves 'belong' in the collective unconscious. From the unconscious they can exert their influence upon the psyche and give valuable guidance in the difficulties with which a man is confronted. Their energy can be channelled into consciousness through the psychic elements which form a complex round them, but if this is not allowed to happen (that is, if one refuses to acknowledge those elements and allow them to play their part) then the power of the archetype is liable to become a danger to oneself and to others.

The most obvious danger has been referred to in an

earlier chapter, and that is the danger of being possessed by an archetype. When this happens the individual who is possessed becomes both more and less
than human. In so far as the power of the archetype is
the power of the unconscious, the individual becomes
more than human and is identified with the archetype;
but in so far as the archetype is only one aspect of human
nature he loses the balancing power of the other archetypes and becomes insensible to a whole range of
human experience. Those who are possessed in this way
become fanatics who have discovered the only final
truth, or the very depths of love, and who seek to force
everyone else into the pattern of the one archetype that
fills the centre of their own life. Direct acquaintance
with the archetypes is fraught with the greatest danger.

Jungian psychology teaches the lesson that we should
try to become aware of the presence of the archetypes
in the unconscious, partly in order that we may allow
them to play their part in our lives and partly in order
that we may guard against the danger of having them
thrust upon us. There is a good reason why this lesson
is especially necessary at the present time. In the past
mankind both came to terms with the archetypes and
disassociated himself from them by projecting them
upon the earth and the sky in the form of gods and
demons. In general, man came to terms with the gods
that he had created for himself by rituals and magic,
but he also knew that gods and demons could possess a
man. Because possession of this kind was 'understood'
(at least by priests and medicine men) it was far less
dangerous than possession by archetypes is today; this
is because the man who was possessed (as he supposed)
by god or demon had no temptation to identify the

power that possessed him with his own ego. Today possession by archetypes is not 'understood' in terms of any generally accepted convention, and those who are possessed are liable to suppose that the powers generated are the powers of their own ego. Now that we have lost the safeguards provided by earlier ideas of gods and demons there is a dangerous vacuum in our thought, and psychotherapy may help to provide a means of coming to terms with the phenomena associated with archetypes.

We should not suppose that it is right to project the archetypes into gods and demons, but it is essential to have some framework of thought within which the actual events to which archetypes give rise can be understood. If one does not they run amok. There are real powers within each one of us that can poison not only our own lives but also the lives of those with whom we live. We favour some and claim them as our own; we reject others and project them upon other people. The most glaring example of this is the gulf between East and West, across which each sees in the other all the evil things he will not see in himself.

9 The Self

The Archetype of Deity

Man has to come to terms with the powers he encounters, whether these powers are in the external world or within the psyche. The advance of science and technology has been a gradual process of coming to terms with the powers that exist outside man, and one result of this has been that we have learnt to distinguish between inner and outer powers in a way that men and women of earlier ages did not. The alchemists, for example, attempted to come to terms with inner and outer powers at the same time by projecting (as we say today) their inner psychic energies upon their external experiments, and ancient peoples thought that the gods might act in men as well as in the world of nature. It is still possible for us to project inner powers outside ourselves into the idea of external gods, but as a result of our scientific approach we do not connect such gods with natural phenomena as men did in the past.

The projection of archetypes into the idea of gods or a God leads to serious errors. When one forms the idea of God according to an inner image or power in the psyche one is giving supreme psychic value to that image or power. For example, if one forms one's idea of God according to the pattern of human consciousness one gives supreme value to consciousness at the expense of the unconscious; if one forms one's idea of God on the model of the archetype of the Magician one gives supreme value to the basic masculine aspect of the psyche. These archetypes are incomplete personalities which stress certain aspects of human nature at the expense of the rest, and if they are projected into the idea of God one finishes up with a limited idea of God and a tendency to reject a large part of the psyche. This is unsatisfactory from both a religious and a psychological point of view. From a religious point of view it means that one is offering worship, respect or devotion to a god who is less complete and more one-sided than a human being; from a psychological point of view it means that one is trying to live with a limited part of one's total nature.

In general, we can no longer safely project the archetypes into the idea of gods, but there is one archetype of which this is not true. This archetype is a sort of 'archetype of archetypes'. Just as the archetypes are the centres of complexes that lie hidden behind the psychic elements grouped around them, so this ultimate archetype is, as it were, the nucleus of the total complex which is the psyche, and it lies hidden within and behind the other archetypes. It could be said that it is the archetype that represents and gives expression to the fact that in each individual man the psychic elements common to all men are organised and related together in a particular way, in order to give rise to that particular individuality. The other archetypes, the ego-complex which is consciousness, and all the psychic elements active in the life of a man can be thought of as partial expressions of this fundamental archetype that lies behind the others.

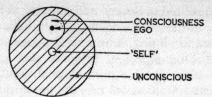

The 'self' is to the totality as the ego is to consciousness

Jung calls this ultimate and central archetype by many names. He calls it 'the Self', and this can lead to confusion if it is not carefully distinguished from '-self', as in 'myself', 'himself' and so on, because these expressions usually refer to consciousness (the 'I' of conscious life) whereas 'the Self' refers to the totality of the psyche, conscious and unconscious. Jung also calls this archetype 'the Image of God' and 'the archetype of Deity', and he tells us that when it is active it expresses itself in ideas and symbols usually connected with the idea of God. He calls it 'the archetype of wholeness' because it becomes visibly effective when an individual is moving towards psychic wholeness and completion, and 'the archetype of unity' because it points to the possibility of living a life in which the psyche functions as a united whole. Little harm need be done either from a religious or from a psychological point of view if the idea of God is formed after the pattern of this archetype.

From a religious point of view the kind of God whom one would accept if one took this archetype as one's pattern is a God in whom all our human problems are resolved, that is one in whom 'all things work together for good'; he is a God who is ultimately responsible for the whole range of natural phenomena, and who is related to the evil and suffering in the world as well as to the good and happiness; he is the One God, united in himself, in whom all things are joined, and there is no aspect of existence that cannot be related to him. From a psychological point of view belief in such a God may or may not be beneficial. It is entirely beneficial if the belief carries with it a real devotion and a real striving towards the fullness of God himself, for such a belief, psychologically understood, involves the ascription of supreme value to the archetype of the Self. On the other hand, if belief in such a God carries with it the idea that God is beyond all human experience, that relationship with him is impossible and that he is so entirely different from man that no striving towards him is possible, then, psychologically understood, it means a rejection of the archetype of the Self for all the practical purposes of living.

We have said that one may 'form' one's idea of God according to the pattern of an archetype. It should be realised that this is not something we do by conscious decision and choice. Our idea of God is something we simply 'have' (or do not have), and we have never sat down to decide just what it shall be. One compares a man's idea of God with an archetype and then speaks of it being formed according to the model of that archetype if the correspondence is sufficiently close.

The Self as Guide

In Chapter 7 we spoke of accepting the 'other side', that is the psychic elements that do not fit in with the pattern of consciousness. We said that all one could do was to hold both sides in consciousness, without giving greater value to either, even though they might seem to be opposed to each other. We also said that one could not make a conscious effort to relate the two sides in order to form a new synthesis but that if one continued to endure the tension between the two sides such a synthesis was ultimately formed. One can observe such a process as this in everyday life, and the instance of the devoted scientist whose life was disturbed by his relationship with a woman was given in Chapter 7; but it is most easily observed when it occurs in the course of a psychological analysis.

In analysis the patient is likely to become aware of the 'other side', and of the conflict between the psychic elements that make it up and his conscious attitude and approach. If this occurs neither the analyst nor the patient is in a position to decide upon a way in which the two sides can be brought together in a synthesis and both need to exercise great patience. It is reported as a fact that in such circumstances the solution of the patient's problem often 'arises', without the conscious planning of the patient or analyst, and that when it does it arises in the form of yet a new psychic element which begins to take charge of the process of development. This 'taking charge' has two aspects. On the one hand, the patient gradually begins to find a new way of living which involves the exercise of both sides of his nature at the same time and, on the other hand, dreams and images occur in his mind that seem to him to have extraordinary power and importance: they have the quality of demanding attention, interest and even submission. It is often the case that both patient and analyst become aware of the presence of a force or power that does not derive from the conscious thought of either of them and is directing the further course of the analysis. It is this power that is understood (in the terms of Analytical Psychology) as a manifestation of the Self.

The images and ideas that arise at such a time not only have the quality of demanding attention but also show features that are related to both sides of the conflict of which the patient is aware. At first sight it seems that the new thing is created out of the opposites that have come into conflict in the patient's mind, and it may well be that this is a valuable way of thinking about the process. It is even more helpful to think of the two sides that are in conflict as aspects of the uniting image or idea which now makes its appearance. In other words, to think of the conflicting elements as partial expressions of the Self which is striving to express itself through them.

The Self takes charge of the process of development when one is ready to admit that one's conscious direction of one's life is not the final answer to the mystery of living and that one must take into account things that seem to contradict one's conscious intention. In other words, the Self takes charge when we give up the claim to have complete control. It hardly needs to be said that there is a close parallel between this psychological idea and the religious idea that God takes charge of our lives when we are willing to submit the direction of them to him alone.

The 'Wrath' of the Self

There are two kinds of guidance and both can be ascribed equally to God and the Self. When a child stretches out his hand towards the fire there comes a point at which the heat becomes really uncomfortable, and the child is hurt. This warning of pain is 'guidance', it guides the child away from the dangerous act of putting his hand in the fire. Christians (and people of many other religions, too) believe that God guides us in this kind of way, as well as by directing our lives if we will let him. In fact, it is suggested that if we do not give up the direction of our lives to God we direct them along wrong paths and so come up against the 'wrath' of God, which, like the child's pain, is intended to turn us away from the wrong direction in which we are going. When one considers the psychological idea of the Self one can regard its behaviour in a very similar way.

We have already pointed out many times that unconscious psychic elements interfere with our conscious plans and purposes and that this is the main reason why we find that we have to take notice of them. In saying this we have so far made no attempt to discuss why this should be so, but it is obvious that the reason is that unconscious psychic elements refer to facts about the totality of our nature which are just as important as the facts we know about in consciousness. The particular form that interference by the unconscious takes depends upon what elements happen to be active in the unconscious, but the possibility of such interference depends upon the fact that the individual is a whole— and it is this fact that is expressed by the idea of the archetype of the Self. This means that the interference with conscious intention by unconscious elements may be regarded as an activity of the Self.

Two illustrations can be given of the way in which the Self can be said to provide the same kind of 'negative guidance' which is ascribed to God when one speaks of his 'wrath'. Suppose a business man has very high sexual moral principles but becomes involved in an affair with his secretary. He makes a conscious decision about this and intends to continue the affair, and in order to do so he has to repress or devalue his sexual morality. We all know the sort of argument by which he does this—he speaks to himself about the importance of personal relationships, the overruling nature of love and the relativity of moral judgements, and he tells himself that he will see to it that his wife does not suffer as a result of his behaviour. His conscious intention is to carry on the affair and to keep it secret from his wife, and in order to carry out this intention he has to put aside one aspect of his own character—his moral principle. If he now finds that he continually gets into emotional tangles and rows with his mistress quite contrary to his intention, this could be regarded as the effect of his repressed morality and as the activity of the Self creating trouble because the man has not acted in accordance with his total nature. It would be an even more glaring example of this if the man was normally very careful but, by a gross act of unnatural carelessness, allowed his wife to find out what was going on.

The second illustration has been mentioned before. If someone refuses to admit that he has 'bad' elements within him and sets out to live a life of extreme virtue, then one of two things is likely to happen. He is likely to find either that he gives way to unexpected tendencies to behave in ways he thinks are deplorable and so suffers torments of guilt, or that he develops a neurosis which interferes continually with his chosen way of life. Such a neurosis can be regarded as a 'compensation' for his attempt to live too narrow a life which does not give opportunities for his total nature to develop, and if the man can be persuaded to see it in this light he may be led to a new approach to life and continuing development.

The unconscious always has a 'compensatory' tendency, and it is always liable to bring to nothing our attempts to live a one-sided life—whether those attempts are made in the interests of personal pleasure or strict virtue. This happens because we are far more than our conscious selves, and one-sidedness is the attempt to ignore this inescapable fact. As we have said, this fact is expressed by the archetype of the Self, and we are correct in saying that compensation by the unconscious which destroys our conscious intentions is the activity of the Self and that this activity is a negative guidance, which can be compared with the religious idea of the 'wrath' of God.

The Self as Creator

The development of consciousness is only possible as the result of the acquisition of new conscious psychic elements (ideas, judgements, attitudes and so on), and it can be understood as the coming into consciousness of things that were previously unconscious. From this point of view the unconscious is a storehouse of psychic elements which become conscious one or two at a time and, from a slightly different point of view, it is the power supply that keeps psychic life going. When we speak of the development of the psyche we assume the existence of a conscious mind, to which the unconscious can make contributions, but consciousness itself is the result of development. A new-born child has no self-consciousness whatsoever, and in the first years of its life the consciousness it possesses is at best intermittent. The development of an organised central consciousness which one thinks of as 'I' is part of the period of early growth and it is not something that one has from the beginning. Consciousness itself must be thought of as 'born' out of the unconscious.

Certain suggestions that Dr. Fordham has made bear upon this. In studying the habit of some young children of drawing circles he came to the conclusion that these circles were connected in the child's mind with 'I', but he also thought that they were hardly representations of the 'I' of ego-consciousness: rather, they represented the totality of the self, with the possibility of the development of the adult 'I' within it. In other words, such circles could be regarded as representations of the Self and as symbols of the protected area in which the development of consciousness could take place.

The development of consciousness from a state of unconsciousness is only possible in so far as the unconscious state is somehow the state of an individual. In other words, from the beginning there is the possibility of individual development inherent in the psyche of a baby, and it seems certain that, however much circumstances may direct the actual course of development, the possibilities latent in the original unconscious state also exert a determining influence. When we think of the Self as an expression of the individual totality of a person we must see the Self as the origin or matrix out of which the conscious individual develops, and when we think of it as the potential wholeness to which the life of an individual may point we must also see it as the directing source that guides the development of consciousness. In this way the Self stands to the conscious individual both as creator and as preserver.

The Self as Goal

The individual mind, in which a developed consciousness rests upon a background of undeveloped unconscious elements, is created by the Self out of the unlimited potential of an original unconscious state. It is also directed towards a complete development in which the total psyche will play its part in the life of the individual. This goal is not to be understood as a final state in which everything has become conscious but rather as a dynamic association between consciousness and the unconscious in which neither has the last word. For this reason it is not a state in which the ego has complete control of everything but one in which the ego takes its proper place, exercises full responsibility for the activity of consciousness and, at the same time, acknowledges the existence of other determining factors in the psyche. In the final analysis it must be said that the ego is subordinate to the direction of something else.

This something else to which the ego is subordinate is not the unconscious, because if this were so the individual's life would be just as one-sided as it would be if it were directed exclusively by consciousness. The ultimate control is carried out by the totality of the psyche, of which ego-consciousness and the unconscious are both partial expressions. Thus the goal of development is to allow the Self to express itself fully in one's life in whatever way it chooses, and thus the Self stands at the end as goal as well as at the beginning as origin and creator.

The Self as a Power

'The Self' can be regarded as an intellectual idea by means of which it is possible to link together a large variety of things that happen in human life. At first sight there is no connection between, say, a dream in which one enters a formal garden and finds at its centre the statue of a Greek god and a disastrous act of foolishness which completely spoils an important venture upon which one happens to be engaged, but by using the idea of the Self one can relate them together. The dream expresses the need to unite the whole of one's personality (represented by the ordered and formal garden) around a controlling centre (represented by the god), and the act of foolishness is a result of neglecting some aspect of one's personality. The Self manifests itself as a goal in the dream, and in 'negative guidance' in the course of waking life.

In this chapter we have tried to show that many different aspects of life can be connected together by this idea and that many of the most important features of life can be connected together as expressions of or attitudes to the Self. Many dreams that we remember as particularly powerful and significant are expressions of the Self, and when we become aware of the insignificance of our own ego-consciousness in comparison with the other powers and forces within the psyche we are taking up an attitude to the Self. As an intellectual idea the Self can best be understood as a way of referring to the essential fact that each one of us is an individual human being, within which manifold powers and possibilities are at work, and which can develop in such a way that these powers and possibilities find expression.

If one talks about the Self in this way to those who have had experience of psychological analysis one might be told 'You don't know what you are talking about; the Self is not just an idea, a concept, it is a real thing, an active power which you can only know by experiencing it'. This claim is partly true and partly false. It is partly false because there is no doubt that the Self is an idea in the mind: the Self is said to express itself in a large number of different ways, and the connection between the ways in which it expresses itself is not given in experience. As the illustration at the beginning of this section shows, we should not imagine that there was a connection between two different things, both of which we say manifest the activity of the Self, if we did not already have the idea of the Self by means of which to connect them. It is important to realise this and to see the extent to which the Self is an intellectual idea or concept, but at the same time it is equally important to understand in what way the Self must be regarded as an active power.

The Self must be thought of as a power as well as an idea, because many of the happenings that are connected together by the idea of the Self are happenings in which we experience the exercise of a power upon us. As a connecting idea the Self has to be treated as the origin of the power which is described as the 'activity of the Self', and hence as itself a source of power. A most important, if not *the* most important, use of the idea of the Self is to enable us to think and talk about experiences that involve a dynamic relation between the ego and other forces acting from within the psyche. The ego finds itself up against, or at least in relationship with, psychic forces which make demands upon it or oppose it as obstructive powers, and this is no mere concept or idea but a fact of human experience. One may try to understand such experience by talking about gods and demons, about the One God who governs the universe and in other ways, and one way in which one can talk about them is provided by the idea of the Self.

The use of the idea of the Self to talk about such experiences is an important mark of the difference between jungian and freudian psychology. In general, classical freudian psychology does not employ the idea of anything as absolute as the Self, and within freudian psychology the experience of psychic forces is understood in terms of individual forces and powers (such as the sexual drive) which can, in principle, be guided and directed by the ego. The account given by jungian psychology involves the idea of the unknown Self which is not under the control of the ego in any way but is itself the ultimate, controlling power within (or around) the psyche. The absolute demand, which is usually connected with moral values but also arises in some people in connection with their choice of profession or way of life, is rooted in the Self, and the search for a 'final succour', a place of security from which to face the dangers of life, is a yearning towards the Self. 'The Self' is the name we give to the ultimate power within the psyche which we ignore at our peril.

We all experience the demands, the guidance and the opposition of the Self at one time or another, but naturally it is only those who have learnt to talk in the language of analytical psychology who refer to such experiences by the use of the term 'the Self'. Others may speak of God, or they may ignore the experiences entirely. This is why the encounter with the Self as a power occurs most frequently in the analytical situation. Not only does that situation aim at releasing the powers of the unconscious, it is only in that situation that the use of the term 'the Self' is to be expected. In such a situation there may come a time when both the analyst and the analysand become aware that they have to reckon with a power directing their work which is not the conscious will of either of them: it is as though a third party had entered into the situation, and it becomes more and more clear that the fruitful outcome of the work depends upon the extent to which doctor and patient can permit this third party to take control. The experience is in some sense reminiscent of that of Nebuchadnezzar when he looked into the burning, fiery furnace in which three men had been thrown and saw them walking alive in the company of a fourth 'like a son of the gods'.

Theory and Practice

The previous chapters of this book have been about
words. Very little has been said about anything which
is not the common experience of every one of us, but a
great deal has been said about the way in which
analytical psychologists use their own special words to
talk about such experience. It is certainly true that by
using these words to talk about experience they put a
new slant upon it—as, for example, the use of the word
'unconscious' provides a new approach to the 'odd
things' (such as dreams) that go on in our lives—but
words alone do not create experience. Our main object
has been to show how the words of psychotherapists tie
up with everyday experience.

In one sense it is an accident that psychological language is tied up with everyday experience, although in
another sense it is inevitable. The surgeon has his own
words to describe the objects within the human body
that he encounters in his surgical work, and these words
are generally not applicable to our daily life. Most of
the time we do not have anything to do with the parts
of the body that are disclosed to the surgeon during an
operation and so have no occasion to talk about them.
The words of psychology were coined in order to speak
about the events that take place in the course of
psychotherapeutic work, and it might have been that

words appropriate for this had little relevance to the sort of things that go on in daily life. However, the psychotherapist has no knife with which to lay open parts of the mind that ought normally to be hidden within, and he can only lay bare the unconscious through the consciousness of the patient, which is the same consciousness with which the patient goes about his everyday life. This is why the psychotherapist's words have application beyond his special work.

It is not to be supposed that in every analysis long discussions are held about archetypes, projection and the other things of which we have spoken. This sort of talk is used when one is talking about psychotherapy, not when one is actually practising it, and it corresponds to medical theory, not to what the doctor says to his patient. Discussion in analysis is concerned with the problems and difficulties of the analysand, not with the theories of the analyst. In order to put what has been said in perspective something must be said about psychotherapy itself, that is about the analytical situation. What is psychological analysis? What happens during an analysis? And what is its purpose?

Analysing

If a person who had had no contact with psychotherapists and psychological analysis were asked 'Who analyses what?' he would probably say 'Well, I suppose the analyst analyses the mind of the patient', and this is what one would expect. But analytical psychologists do not talk in this way. The patient says, 'I am analysing' and he may say, 'I am analysing with So-and-so'. The doctor is the analyst, but he does not say that he

analyses his patient because he knows that it is the
patient who is doing the work. The doctor may make a
brilliantly true diagnosis of the patient's troubles; he
may analyse the situation perfectly; but so long as it is
only his idea—that is, so long as the patient does not
agree with what the doctor thinks or says—nothing of
any importance has happened. The patient does the
work with the help of the doctor. Comparing some
forms of psychotherapy with a full analysis an analyst
said, 'That is telling the patient what he ought to know,
analysis is spending years helping the patient to find out
for himself what he ought to know'.

A Personal Relationship

Classical freudian psychology (Psychoanalysis) still
tends to work with the idea derived from medicine that
a doctor does something for the patient, and in a
freudian analysis the doctor stands apart (so far as he
can) in order to bring a detached attitude to his
patient's problems. Whether it is possible for the
analyst to do this is a matter of opinion, and Jung
insists that, whether or not it can be done, it is a mistake. According to Jung, the relationship formed
during analysis is one in which the analyst enters into a
personal relationship with the patient and in which the
analyst is ready to throw his whole personality into the
work.

This personal relationship that forms the analytical
situation is different from the usual relationships between people in two ways. The first difference is that it
is deliberately intended to be a relationship of 'openness' and 'acceptance', and it is this that gives it its

curative power. In most personal relationships there is, quite properly, an element of reserve: one takes note of the character and tastes of the other person involved, and one does not (if one can help it) do or say things that cause distress to him (or her); on the other side, one expects a certain consideration for one's own views. There are also few people who are ready to expose themselves 'naked', as it were, to someone else, and this also sets up a barrier in our relationships. The basic principle of the analyst is that nothing the patient says or does shall break the relationship, and the patient must know (or learn in the course of analysis) that, however open and unreserved he may be in his self-exposure, he will be accepted by the analyst. This openness and acceptance can be a revelation to many people, and it is a most important mark of the analytical situation. The other way in which the relationship differs from most personal relationships is that it is itself an important topic of discussion between the two people who form it.

To a large extent the patient learns about himself and his relationship to other people by examining his relationship with the analyst, but in so far as a true personal relationship has been formed it is not only the patient who contributes to its character: the relationship depends upon the analyst as much as it does upon the patient. This means that the patient cannot form much of an idea about what he has contributed to it unless he also knows a great deal about what the analyst has contributed, and the analyst must help him by attempting to show him this. As a result, the analyst must examine his relationship to the patient in order to enable the patient to examine his relationship to the analyst. For example, the patient may well find that he is treating the analyst very much as though he were his father, and it will be very important for him to discover why he is doing this and how far he is trying to get from the analyst something that he failed to get from his natural father. In such a situation there will be a strong tendency for the analyst to treat the patient as a son or daughter, and even to expect from the patient something that he missed in his relations with his own children, and it is absolutely essential that the analyst should be aware of this and either ensure that he does not fall into the rôle of father or, if he cannot or does not think he should do this, to make sure that the patient knows what is going on. This, of course, is a very elementary example, which applies in some way to the majority of analytical situations.

The jungian attitude to the nature of the analytical relationship grew out of the experience of analysts, but it is very easy to give a theoretical justification of it. A doctor who is dealing with a physical disease is concerned with the functioning of the body, and to a large extent the body of an individual functions in the same way wherever he happens to be. This is not to deny that the mental state of a patient influences his physical state, but although this is true a diseased liver, for example, is not greatly affected by removing a man from his home to an hospital: the physician or surgeon is generally able to treat the body in isolation from the relationships the patient has with other people and with the doctor. The psychological analyst, on the other hand, is dealing with the personality of his patient, and the human personality is not something that can be isolated from personal relationships—it is largely formed by the personal relationships in which the individual has been involved, and it is almost entirely expressed within personal relationships. It follows that any dealings with a patient that involve his personality must also involve the relationships that the individual forms, and it is only if the analyst can work within a real personal relationship that he can hope to give the patient any real help in the work of understanding his psyche.

Projection and the Transference

Projection inevitably plays an important rôle in analysis, and it is often only by projecting unconscious elements upon the analyst that the patient discovers their existence. At the same time, it is very probable that every close personal relationship involves a great deal of projection. The difference is that analysis provides the opportunity of examining what is going on, so that the analytical relationship becomes a special relationship which throws light upon all personal relationships. Many ordinary relationships would be irreparably damaged if one had to examine them in the same way as patient and analyst examine their relationships within the analytical situation.

The patient projects upon the analyst elements of his own psyche of which he is not aware, and he then relates to the analyst as though that element were a personal characteristic of the analyst. For example, suppose that the patient has always tried to be 'broadminded' and not to take a critical attitude to the behaviour of other people. This may mean that he has repressed a considerable tendency to criticise others and that in order to be broad-minded he has had to fight the temptation to behave like a prim old maid. In such a case the patient may project his old-maidishness upon the analyst, and this sets up a relationship between patient and analyst characterised by a tendency for the analyst to disapprove of the patient, or, at least, to seem to the patient to disapprove of him. In such a situation one of two things happens. If the analyst accepts the rôle of disapproving critic (which is something one would not expect him to do), then he does actually experience disapproval of the things that the patient (unconsciously) wants him to disapprove of, and the patient gets a great kick out of coming and talking about such things so that they can be condemned. In such a situation nothing gets done and analysis drags on without doing anyone any good. The function of the analyst is to be aware of what is going on and to refuse to let his real opinions be distorted by projection, so that he can gradually enable the patient to distinguish between what he actually thinks and what he (the patient) has projected upon him. In this way the patient eventually comes to see that the tendency to be critical and old-maidish is his own and that without giving up his broad-mindedness he must somehow make room for this other side. Incidentally, there are as many people who are just as unwilling to accept and come to terms with attitudes like this as there are those who will not acknowledge their unconscious sexual desires.

It should be clearly understood that there is rarely anything crude about projection and that it is a subtle happening which it requires long training to spot. The patient does not normally project just anything on the analyst, he projects things that are appropriate to the particular analyst with whom he is involved. In other words, the projection tends to bring out aspects of the analyst's character, and this is why it is only after long training that an analyst is able to distinguish between his own attitude and the attitude that the patient projects upon him. The importance of doing this may lead the analyst into the opposite error: since he is on his guard against accepting the attitude that the patient projects upon him he may falsify his own attitude as a result. For example, if the patient is attempting to project a disapproving attitude upon the analyst, the analyst may be in danger of hiding his own real disapproval in order to compensate for the effects of projection, and this can falsify the relationship just as much as the projection itself. The analyst must accept the patient, whatever the patient may say, but this does not mean that he must agree that the patient is right in everything that he does.

'Transference' is a special and very important case of projection, and it plays an important part in very many analytical situations. A transference occurs when the patient projects upon the analyst characteristics that he has, in the past, attributed to his parents (or parent) and so takes to the analyst the attitude that he took to his parents as a child. The main reasons why this should be a fairly common feature of analysis are obvious: first, there is a real parallel between the parent–child relationship and the analyst–patient relationship, because in both one is seeking help and support from the other; secondly, there are large numbers of people whose mental difficulties originated in their childhood and whose present mental disturbance is due to a failure to enter into proper relationship with their parents in the past. The transference situation in the analysis enables people to recover the problems of their childhood and then to attempt to deal with them in an adult manner.

The transference is said to be either 'positive' or 'negative', and this is ultimately a reflection of the fact that our attitude to our parents is inevitably two-sided. On the one hand, it is essential that the growing child should depend both physically and psychically upon his parents: he must rely upon them for physical necessities, for love and companionship, and for direction and guidance; and this is the aspect of the parent–child relationship that is repeated when a positive transference to the analyst sets in. On the other hand, the growing child has also to learn to stand on his own feet, to provide his own necessities, to form his own ideas and opinions and to live his own life. In his attempt to do this his parents stand in his way, and they do this whether they themselves try to keep their child dependent upon them or not: to the growing child they represent security and safety from the dangers of life, and he can only learn to live his own life if he is ready to give up the security which they offer, so that, even if he does not have to fight against his actual parents in order to free himself, he still has to fight against his own desire for their continued protection and guidance. From this point of view the parents represent hated enemies which prevent a man from living his own life and, at the same time, enemies from whom he cannot bear to disassociate himself; this is the aspect of the parent–child relationship that is reflected in a negative transference.

When a positive transference is formed, the patient

appears completely dependent upon the analyst; he is unwilling to think for himself and appears to listen carefully and intelligently to all that the analyst says. He tries to please the analyst in every way. This appears to be delightful from the analyst's point of view, but, in fact, it is not at all a satisfactory state of affairs and is liable to make nonsense of the whole analysis. The purpose of analysis is not to teach the patient one or two useful ideas and habits but to enable the patient to live his own life as fully as he can. In order to make real use of a positive transference the analyst has to set the patient on his own feet, and he has to do it without withdrawing himself from the patient in such a way that he creates the same emotional shock as that which results from the loss or withdrawal of a loved parent. If a negative transference is formed the patient does not usually leave the analyst, because it reflects the situation in which the child cannot bring himself to leave the security offered by his parents; but although he insists upon continuing the work he violently rejects all that the analyst is and says. In many ways this situation provides a more hopeful basis for useful work than a positive transference, because the patient is, at least, trying to form ideas of his own in opposition to those of the analyst. It is not to be thought that analysis cannot be carried out without a transference forming, but it is a fact that it is formed in a large number of analytical situations.

Analysis is the creation of a situation in which things happen within a personal relationship, and in which the things that happen can be watched and examined. For instance, in normal situations one may feel anger and contempt towards someone else, and the result of this is to poison one's relationship with that person, to cause him to defend himself and to take up an equally aggressive attitude; this, in turn, confirms one in one's attitude to him and destroys all hope of a profitable relationship. Within analysis, if one feels and expresses anger and contempt towards the analyst he does not defend himself by aggressive attitudes or rebuff one but forces one to examine one's own attitude and eventually to seek out the origin of it in oneself. This examination and discussion of one's attitude depends upon two things: it depends upon the readiness of the analyst to accept whatever attitude one takes up and also upon one's own readiness to think about what one is doing. In everyday life it is rare for both these things to apply. It is certainly possible for a person to accept the antagonism of someone else (it is the meaning of Jesus' instruction about 'turning the other cheek') and such acceptance certainly has helpful results; unfortunately, it does not often happen that when one person is able to accept the antagonism of another the other is ready to subject his antagonism to careful examination.

It should be obvious that the work of an analyst is beset by difficulties and dangers. However much training he has had, and for however long he has himself analysed, he remains a human being with his own unconscious character and his own repressions. In accepting a personal relationship with his patient he is exposing both himself and his patient to the forces that exist in the unconscious on either side, and these forces can be powerful and dangerous.

The Aim of the Analyst

It is natural that one should ask 'What is an analyst trying to do?' and most people who try to get an answer to this question soon experience great frustration. At the beginning the patient knows well enough what he expects from analysing, and that is to get rid of the symptoms that disturb him, but the analyst has a rather different attitude to the work. From the point of view of the analyst the symptoms of the patient are symptoms of a general *malaise* of the psyche, and the analyst is concerned with the psychic development of the patient, not with particular problems that seem important to the patient—naturally he has to follow the patient in his account of his symptoms and in his description of his immediate problems, but he also expects to find that the patient's real problems are hidden even from the patient and that they will only come into the open in the course of the work. It may happen that after a period the patient's symptoms disappear and that he wishes to stop analysing, but this is comparatively rare. It is more common for the patient to find that he is bound to the analytical work and unready to give it up long after he has ceased to be concerned with his original symptoms.

The analyst does not start with the idea of this or that goal to which he hopes to bring the patient. His attitude is, rather, that there are psychic forces at work within the patient's psyche, that it is because of these forces that the patient has been brought to analysis and that the object of analysis is to co-operate with them. The analyst's contribution to the work is not to direct the patient's development but to help the patient to set aside the conscious restrictions and blocks that prevent the forces within him from guiding him in the right way. The analyst does not think of himself as someone in possession of all the answers to the patient's problem but as someone who has been called to help the patient and who is ready to do so to the best of his ability—wherever it is that the patient is going. As with all professions there are some who become analysts for wrong reasons, but it is clear that the right reason is that a man has been led to take up the work of an analyst by forces beyond his conscious control. Having been led to this work he is then called upon to help this or that particular patient. What effect his help will have he does not know.

There is no such thing as an analysis that has come to a 'successful conclusion', there are only analytical situations that have come to an end—possibly because the particular analyst has given the patient all the help that he can, possibly because something has gone wrong with the relationship. Ideally, an analysis continues so long as things are going on, that is as long as the relationship between analyst and patient develops, and the patient discovers more about himself. It may well happen that the relationship gets into a groove and that, even so, the patient insists upon maintaining it. In such a case the patient may be right and a long fallow period may be necessary before further development can take place, or it may be that he is wrong and that the analysis (with that analyst) should stop. There is no way of settling such questions beforehand, and analyst and patient must judge as best they can; all that one can really say is that an analysis goes on until it stops. One can also say that most people who have taken analysis seriously over a longish period of time have discovered a new approach to living which enables them to deal more adequately with the problems that are set by their encounters with other people.

Epilogue: An Impression of Jungianism

Some years ago I was speaking to a jungian analyst about the use of a couch in analysis and I was told that in many cases there were things that could not be reached without it. Within a few weeks another analyst remarked that he had no couch in his consulting room: 'I did have one before I moved,' he said, 'but no one ever used it so there didn't seem much point.' The two people concerned were both Jungians with considerable respect for each other, and I tell this rather silly story to show how impossible it is to generalise about jungian ideas or jungian practice. The idea that there is one and only one right way for everybody is directly contrary to the spirit of Jung's thought and of Jungianism. One cannot point to a system or a method and say 'this is Analytical Psychology', and this is one reason why one cannot describe a process of development and say 'this is how Analytical Psychology has developed'.

The wide range of differing views among analytical psychologists is only one reason for this. An equally important reason is that the practice of Analytical Psychology is only one aspect of what one might call Jungianism. As with so much else this goes back to Jung himself. One has only to glance through his books to see the extent to which his thought moved over fields

far removed from the consulting room, even though
that is where he began and that is where he returned
again and again. His thought and his investigations
ranged over the world religions, ancient myths and
legends, medieval alchemy, modern tribal customs; he
wrote about the Bible (*Answer to Job*), flying saucers,
parapsychology and a host of other things. He was
concerned with everything that has emerged from the
mind of man and his ideas have relevance to all human
activity as well as to the practice of analysis. The
attempt to describe how Jungianism has developed
would require one to trace the influence of Jung's ideas
over an enormous range—to give only one example, the
operas of Michael Tippett are directly influenced by
jungian thought.

Jungianism is far more a mode of thinking, an
approach to life than anything else, and when I was
asked to add a final chapter on 'later developments' I
knew that, so far as I was concerned, the task was impossible. Failing that, all I can give is a kind of
personal appraisal, a purely individual account of what
I think Jungianism is about.

'Dominating my interests and research was the burning
question: "what actually takes place inside the mentally ill".'[1] That is how Jung opens his account of his
psychiatric studies, and in one sense this means that he
was not primarily a therapist. I do not, of course, mean
that he was not a therapist but that therapy was not his
only concern. One could give an illustration from a
wholly different activity, that of a motor mechanic.
How often I have been infuriated when something has

[1] *Memories, Dreams and Reflections*, p. 116.

gone wrong with my car, the mechanic puts it right and then cannot tell me what was wrong! Yet the mechanic has done the job he was asked to do and the important thing is that the car now works properly. Another mechanic will want to know what actually happened inside the works, what went wrong, how he put it right. 'But,' it may be said, 'this wanting to know, this need to learn is really part of the job of putting right; the mechanic who wants to understand only wants to understand in order to be a better mechanic, to be able to put other cars right when they go wrong' and, of course, this is true, but it is also the point of what I am saying. To the psychotherapist whose primary and overriding concern is helping and healing theories about what takes place inside human beings are only of secondary interest; their sole purpose is to help in therapy. But for Jung it was not so. His 'burning question' was clearly something more than a wish to equip himself as fully as possible for therapeutic work; it was a question in its own right and was to spread from 'what actually takes place inside the mentally ill?' to 'what takes place in the human psyche?', a question that lay behind all that he did.

There is another sense in which Jung was not just a therapist as the word is usually understood. In psychology 'health' is a very difficult word to define, but probably the majority of people seeking therapy want to be rid of some kind of mental disturbance and be able to live what they think of as a 'normal' life. Once again, it is not that Jung was not able or concerned to help in this way, but it was far from being his leading interest. When he writes of his patients he does so with enormous respect, but in one instance he comes very near to contempt; this is when he writes of a 'normal' man, a doctor of whom he says, 'Now he had a normal practice, normal success, a normal wife, normal children, lived in a normal little house in a normal little town, had a normal income and probably a normal diet,' and, after explaining how they were both glad to bring his analysis to an end, he ends up 'Immediately afterwards he returned home. He never again stirred up the unconscious. His emphatic normality reflected a personality which would not have been developed but simply shattered by a confrontation with the unconscious.'[1] Jung confessed that, whatever help he might give others, his eye followed those who were able and ready to develop as a result of an encounter with the unconscious, those who through analysis could come to begin to activate potentialities hidden within them.

This attitude to his work was closely associated with Jung's unwavering stress upon the individual. He frequently points out that on a beach of pebbles there is an average size and weight for those pebbles, and yet it may be that no single pebble is actually that size or that weight. There are times when he almost uses 'average' and 'normal' as though they were dirty words. As Jung saw it each man has his own 'life-myth', and as he passes through life so he lives out his own, particular myth. His writings suggest that in his opinion no one has any choice about this; whether we want to or not we must, perforce, live out our myth, and yet, at the same time, we have an enormously significant choice. The choice we are confronted with is whether we will accept our myth and live it out as knowingly and as consciously as we can, or whether we

[1] ibid., pp. 133, 135.

will reject it and seek to follow a pattern of our own conscious choosing. In the second case we do not so much live out our myth, but it lives us against our will and the result is confusion and distress. Neumann had this idea in mind when he claimed that Oedipus was not a true hero because he did not know what he was doing when he killed his father, nor when he married his mother: that his self-blinding was, as it were, an acknowledgement of the blindness that had been with him from the beginning.[1]

Jung's emphasis on the individual and the particular development appropriate to each individual remains an important element in Jungianism and in the attitude of jungian analysts. It is given expression in the recorded words of a patient who said, 'I now see that I did not come to analysis because I got claustrophobia, I got claustrophobia in order to be brought into analysis'.[2] In other words, the symptom, the disturbance which at first one seeks to be rid of as a source of irritation and distress comes to be seen as a signpost, a pointer to some other, more far-reaching need, and this means that the aim and purpose of analysis is seen as something much more than just getting rid of the cause of distress. It is the wider aim of integration, or individuation.

It is inevitable that within the field of therapy the emphasis should shift. The analyst is a healer by calling and there are many, many more people who are in need of re-establishment and of moderating or learning to live with mental disturbance than there are who are capable of facing the full task of encountering the un-

[1] Erich Neumann: *The Origins and History of Consciousness*, p. 163.
[2] See Gerhard Adler: *The Living Symbol*.

conscious and developing their deeper potentialities. Even if there were no other consideration it would be impossible to pass such people by on the other side, but if altrusim and concern should fail there is another pressure. The analyst is not only following a calling, he also has to earn his living, and he is in no position to turn away a large proportion of those who come to him because they are not able to go as far as he would like and, anyway, how would he know which were which until 'afterwards'? Nevertheless, within Jungianism the overarching idea of developing one's own, individual personality remains a hope, even when it cannot always be an actual aim.

In keeping with his sense of the individual and his rejection of the average and the normal Jung did not offer a method of analysis, nor even a system of psychology. His own claim, which he made again and again, was that he recorded what he observed and avoided theory and system. He drew his material from personal observation of, for example, African tribes, from old and obscure books and manuscripts, from what went on in his own mind as well as from his experience of patients. So concerned was he to establish the empirical nature of his work that there are times in his books when the lists of relevant happenings and records go on for so long that they not only put the reader off but also obscure the underlying framework. Nevertheless, the framework is always there because, in the last analysis, the matters he recorded were those that he chose to record and they are set within the framework of his own thinking. It is this framework that gives Jungianism its attitude, its viewpoint, its peculiar flavour.

As with his thought, so with his analytical work. He

said 'the man is his method', and he insisted that the
supreme thing the doctor brought to his work was his
own personality and his care for the patient. In one
sense he meant that the therapist must have no method,
but only in the very special sense in which that means
that he must have (if it were possible) all methods. He
did not intend to free the analyst from the use of
method but to free him to use whatever method might
be appropriate: that, knowing methods, being experi-
enced in the use of methods, the analyst should respond
as a person to the analytical situation. 'If the reader
should conclude that little or nothing lay in the
method,' he wrote, 'I would regard that as a total mis-
apprehension of my meaning.'[1] Yet the method remains subordinate to the personality of the analyst—
and to that of the patient. For this reason, it should be
impossible to say of a particular analyst 'This is how X
works'. It may be that X worked in this or that way
with you, that he was almost invariably silent, listened
to dreams without offering interpretations, or that he
spoke what seemed overmuch and had some comment
to make on nearly every dream, but whatever it was
you would have no assurance that this was how he
worked with all patients; you would only know that X,
being X, worked in that way with you, you being who
you were, with your particular problems. Not only
does the analyst bring his personality to the analysis but
also every analytical relationship between two people is
unique and gives rise to a style appropriate to it in its
uniqueness.

We can say the same thing about the uniqueness of
the analytical relationship as we said about the life-

[1] *The Practice of Psychotherapy*, p. 138.

myth of the individual—it is not something consciously chosen but something that happens whether we like it or not. All one can do is to choose whether to acknowledge the fact and welcome it, not only as a challenge but also as an important element in the analytical work, or to try to deny it and treat it as a snare and a hindrance. The analyst who follows a clear-cut, strict method, who attempts rigorously to 'be the same' to every patient, who insists that there is one right way of doing the work which he attempts to follow at all times is acting according to his own personality and impelled by his need of the support he gets from knowing and following the received way; what he is not doing is keeping his own personality out of the relationship, and if he thinks that he is then he is using his method to hide from himself the extent to which his own personality contributes to the work.

Rightly or wrongly, Jung thought Freud's couch was a protective and defensive device to screen out the analyst's personality and avoid the counter-transference. He wrote 'Freud had already discovered the phenomenon of the "counter-transference". Those acquainted with his technique will be aware of its marked tendency to keep the person of the doctor as far as possible beyond the reach of this effect. Hence the doctor's preference for sitting behind the patient, also his pretence that the transference is a product of his technique . . .'[1] In this context Jung's own preference for sitting face to face with his patient can be seen as a way of giving expression to the reality of the situation, the reality of an encounter between two people in which both play an active role and to which both contribute.

[1] ibid., p. 171.

This idea of an encounter to which both participants contribute gives rise to another feature of the jungian approach. This is the idea of a 'third'. When two people meet we have to consider what goes on *between* them, as well as what goes on in each of them, and what lies between them is neither the one nor the other, nor both, but a third. This idea also gives an opportunity to indicate, once again, the enormous range of jungian thought. In itself the idea is simple and even obvious enough, and it is probable that most Jungians (I would not dare say 'all') would agree that it was true and important, and yet this one idea can crop up in a tremendous number of different forms. At the one end of the scale it need be taken to mean no more than that there is an enormous adjustment made between analyst and patient so that each, in the presence of the other, is subtly different from what he would be with anyone else. It can be taken to mean that a work lies between the two and that all that each does is concerned with the work common to them both. Or, at the other end of the scale, it can be taken to mean that there is some overriding meaning or purpose beyond the conscious intention of either participant which each, in some way, serves. Very much as unknown archetypes are expressed through a variety of archetypal images, so the unknown third is given conscious expression and meaning in a variety of accounts of what it means.

Despite Jung's strictures on the technique of Freud, if I were to walk into the consulting room of an analytical psychologist in London I should expect to find a couch. I should expect the analyst's chair to be strategically placed in such a way that it was equally convenient whether the patient were to sit in a chair or to lie upon

the couch. Sitting in the chair the patient would not
be directly facing the analyst but looking, as it were,
across, just in front of him, so that with a very small
movement he could look directly at him. Lying on the
couch the patient would also be able to look at the
analyst if he wished, but he would have no need to.
This, I say, is what I would expect, but I have no doubt
that in many such consulting rooms my expectations
would prove wrong! I would also expect, and would
regard it as the jungian thing, that if a patient were to
walk in it would be left to him whether he sat upon the
chair or lay upon the couch—I do not mean, of course,
that he would be *asked* which he preferred but rather
that he would be left to do whatever he did do.[1] When
an analysis was well-established the analyst might
suggest a move from chair to couch—or vice versa—but
would still leave the choice to the patient, although
analysts would vary greatly in the weight they would
give to such a suggestion.

Whether or not Jung was right in regarding Freud's
use of the couch as a defensive device it is certainly not
in this sense that it has become common among
Jungians. Its use is to be understood in connection with
an outstanding event that occurred in London and that
could well be regarded as traumatic. This was the
impact of the work of Melanie Klein, Winnicott and
Fairburn, all writing from a freudian background,

[1] Perhaps this is a good place to point out that it is not only
Jungians who do jungian things! And that some who do things
that I here call jungian would not call them that themselves. I
can only repeat that Jungianism is not this or that system but an
attitude and that in this chapter I am simply selecting certain of
the elements that go to make up that attitude.

upon members of the Society of Analytical Psychology in London, and this, in turn, was related to another tendency in Jung's own approach.

It is well known that Freud gave enormous importance to the early years of an individual's life, with special emphasis on the development of sexual feeling and interest. Jung never actually denied the importance of the early period and yet he had a tendency to pass over it somewhat lightly. It was not that he ignored it, nor that he did not agree that in many cases the careful analysis of early development might be essential, and yet, at the same time, he managed to give the impression that there were many far more important things in analysis. He described Freud's technique as 'reductive' and regarded it as a kind of unfortunate necessity, something that might have to be done in order to prepare the way for what really mattered. Although Jung stressed the individual he tended to do this in relation to collective, primitive and archetypal material rather than in relation to the detail of personal life. This tendency can be seen in a story he tells in *Memories, Dreams and Reflections*.[1] Jung had dreamt of 'his house' and, in his dream, he had investigated it, starting at the well-furnished upper storey and finishing up under the cellar in a cave where 'were scattered bones and broken pottery, like remains of primitive culture'. There he discovered two human skulls. He recounted this dream to Freud, and Freud pressed him again and again about the skulls because, Jung says, he was interested in the secret death-wishes in the dream. With some naïvety Jung then says that because he wanted to see what would happen he told Freud a lie

[1] pp. 155 f.

and identified the skulls as those of his newly-married wife and his sister-in-law, even though he 'knew perfectly well that there was nothing in myself which pointed to such wishes'. Into his own interpretation of the dream, he said, Freud could not possibly enter. To Jung the dream presented a picture of the psyche, consciousness being represented by the upper storey, and by the lowest part of the house 'the primitive psyche of man' which 'borders on the life of the animal soul, just as the caves of prehistoric times were usually inhabited by animals before men lay claim to them'.

The tendency to stress the infantile personal is a question of emphasis more than anything else. Common ground would be the idea that there is an infant within every adult, but this agreed fact might be approached in two rather different ways. On the one hand, there might be the idea that the prime work was to care for the infant, unravel the tangles that had damaged its development and give it the support and concern necessary if it were to establish itself and grow. On the other hand, there might be the idea that the work was primarily concerned with the adult, yet this second idea would not mean ignoring the infant inside, but rather that that infant was one of whom the adult needed to become aware, relate to and, if necessary, nurture and cherish himself. Not only is the difference more one of approach than anything else, it is also obvious that either approach might be wholly unsuitable in a particular case—as we have said, the work of analysis varies in character from patient to patient as much as it does from analyst to analyst.

The very much greater importance that London

Jungians came to give to the personal, infantile history, and the attempt to recapture infantile attitudes, meant that for many of them the idea of a face-to-face encounter was not appropriate at all stages of the analysis. In so far as it is hoped that the patient will enter into the infantile situation, to that extent he needs to be held, supported, able to let go. Sitting face to face with the analyst he must, to some extent, consciously take up a position and take part in a relationship; lying on the couch he may more easily recapture the inadequacy and almost complete dependence of the infant. The couch is thus seen as a positive aid to the patient, enabling him to discover and explore areas that are blocked by the need to support oneself and to take some kind of conscious control, and not in any sense as a protection for the analyst.

The stress on the collective, the primitive and the archetypal, with its somewhat light concern with the minutiae of personal development, was frequently associated with, though not essentially related to, a kind of jungian 'mystique'. I associate this with some of the post-kantian German philosophers and the impression they sometimes give of being lost in a misty German forest surrounded by denizens of another world. If one is not careful one finds oneself among animas and shadows, animuses and magicians, devouring mothers and wise old men bearing the torch of the logos leaping around in a ritual dance. One feels that a secret and ritual language is being spoken. At its best, language of this kind is a useful shorthand, a means of communication between people who know the language and understand what lies behind the words and, above all, know how to relate the language to what actually happens in people's lives. At its worst, it can be pretentious, obscurantist and even downright nasty.

In many ways Melanie Klein and others offered an opposite extreme to these aspects of Jungianism. Her emphasis was upon the very earliest period of all, the first nine months or so of life and the relationship between the infant and its mother, which meant, to a large extent, the relationship between the infant and its mother's breast. The 'personal' (if a new-born infant can be properly termed a 'person') experience in this earliest period of all was regarded as having overriding importance for all later development, since it was then that the fundamental patterns of living in relationship were laid down and since, moreover, the adult was found again and again to be still reacting in an infantile way to situations of pain and stress. Instead of the language of jungian mystique these ideas were associated with quite another language, supposedly factual and down-to-earth. One spoke of 'real' things, like breasts and sucking and ingesting food and being sick, about introjecting good breasts and rejecting bad breasts, or being poisoned by them and so on. The Kleinian would undoubtedly claim a straightforward, down-to-earth approach, and yet it soon becomes apparent that a good dose of symbolism has crept in. In the end one can only say the same as one said before, that, so far as the language is concerned, it is a valuable shorthand for those who know how to use it but that, at its worst, it can become as obscurantist as and even nastier than the other.

However much one may speak of it being mainly a matter of differences of approach and shifts of emphasis, the introduction of kleinian ideas into jungian thought involved a real opposition, and yet it was an opposition that took place within the framework of Jungianism. There was strain and disagreement, but it is a measure of the width and flexibility of Jungianism that a split was avoided. Even if one might have heard mutters about kleinian Jungians and jungian Jungians, the very phrases were an acknowledgement that both groups were Jungians. It may be that some from London, looking back, would say that, although they very nearly became 'heretics', they finished up as the acknowledged vanguard of Jungianism—though that does not mean that Jungians in Zürich would accept the claim without reservation!

The avoidance of a split was in keeping with the spirit of Jung's thought, since the idea of 'the opposites' and their eventual integration has always been central in it. For example, when it had become clear that his approach was different from that of Freud and others Jung repeatedly presented his position as one that did justice to the stress on sexuality made by Freud and the ideas of power and dominance which were important to Adler and which, doing justice to both, went beyond both. In one place, having described the other two views at considerable length, Jung wrote, 'One cannot simply lay the two explanations side by side, for they contradict each other absolutely,'[1] and 'both theories are in a large measure correct,'[2] and 'The incompatibility of the two theories . . . requires a standpoint superordinate to both, in which they could come together in unison'.[3] There are a great many other places in which

[1] *Two Essays on Analytical Psychology*, p. 39.

[2] ibid., p. 40.

[3] loc. cit.

he writes to the same effect and indicates that he
believes his own standpoint to stand in the reconciling
position with regard to the other two. It is doubtful
whether there is any volume of his collected works in
which 'opposites' does not figure largely in the index.
In *Mysterium Conjunctionis* the reader is confronted with
page after page of paired opposites of one kind and
another. Jung repeatedly presents consciousness and
the unconscious as 'opposites' which at times oppose, at
times compliment or compensate each other. The idea
of the opposites and their eventual integration is central
in all jungian attitudes.

Above all, Jung continually stresses the need to
recognise and accept the 'opposites' in personal life and
personal development, and in practice this means
recognising the side of oneself that has not developed,
the rejected, inferior, dark, evil side which Jung named
'the shadow'. At the heart of all Jung's thinking lies the
conviction that all that is is part of a totality (whether in
the macrocosm or in the microcosm which is a man)
and that to reject or to destroy anything that is there is
to damage or maim the totality, not to purify it.[1]
Pearls of great price are hidden in the dung and, from
another point of view, who are we to judge what has
value and what has not? Always, in jungian thought,
the unconscious is seen as a source or well from which
come things of great value and the seeds of new
creation. It may be desperately dangerous if it is treated

---

[1] This does not mean that there are no situations in which such
action is necessary. It does mean that, if it is necessary, it is an unfortunate necessity and that it should not be taken without awareness of what one is at. Above all, it should not be made into a
virtue.

in the wrong way, but only in co-operation with it can one hope to achieve any worthwhile thing. This same, central idea gives the 'flavour' to jungian analysis; ultimately it is the attempt to activate the opposites and hold them in relation to each other. 'The point,' wrote Jung, 'is not conversion into the opposite but conservation of previous values together with the recognition of their opposites,' he adds, 'naturally this means conflict and self-division'.[1] It is out of such conflict, he is convinced, that in a way which defies both reason and common sense something new creates itself, a superordinate in which the opposites can come together in unison.

The need to accept the totality as it is presented to us, not as we should like it to be and, above all, not as we think it ought to be, is a lesson most of us find very hard to learn. It does not mean that we must stop making moral judgements, nor that we should blur the distinction between what we call evil and what we call good; nor does it mean that we dare not act upon our own judgements. It means to hold to our own notion of good and evil and admit others' rights to hold the opposite view; to maintain the distinction between good and evil in all its sharpness and yet to acknowledge that what we see as evil is as much a part of, and has its place in, the totality as is and does what we see as good; to act according to one's own judgement and yet to know that one's own judgement has no claim to be in accordance with any final or ultimate truth. Some such attitude as this is the first step on the path which, according to Jung, leads to integration and individuation.

[1] ibid., p. 75.

Bibliographical Notes

This is not a 'bibliography' in any strict sense: it is a highly selective choice of a few books and a choice largely directed by personal interest. They are not even all in print.

1 In the Beginning

The three popular classics are

The Interpretation of Dreams
The New Interpretation of Dreams
The Psychopathology of Everyday Life

all by Freud. They may read a bit archaic to us now, but they lay a foundation and establish an approach which, in its broad outline, remains.

2 Jung

(a) *The Time of the Break*

The Psychology of the Unconscious

This has been revised for the Collected Edition of Jung's works and the revised text appears as:

Symbols of Transformation—Vol. 5. Collected Edition

which is a different and, no doubt, a better book—but of far less historical interest.

Jung regarded the publication of the earlier version as the open declaration of his disagreement with Freud's central views. He knew, he said, that Freud could not possibly accept it. Inevitably today it seems the most Freudian of all Jung's writings and for this reason it (the first version) has special interest.

Psychological Types (Routledge & Kegan Paul 1949—first published 1923)

This also, Jung tells us, sprang out of the period of the break. He says that he was led to the study of 'types' by his realisation that he, Freud and Adler produced different ideas and theories because of fundamental differences in their psychological make-up.

The book itself supports its own thesis because, true to type, Jung appears to lose sight of the original problem and become fascinated by and immersed in the general enquiry for its own sake.

It is an important book, especially for those who want to know what Jung himself meant by 'introversion' before the idea was trivialised by the statistical psychologists.

(b) *Introductory*
If one is going to be gripped and fascinated by Jung's writings it does not much matter where one starts. For someone who wants a fairly short, concise and understandable introduction to his ideas in his own words I would suggest

Two Essays in Analytical Psychology—Vol. 7 Collected
   Edition

The well-known *Modern Man in Search of a Soul* is really
too popular to give a true impression.

For those interested in the man as well as his writings
the nearest thing to an autobiography is

Memories, Dreams and Impressions (Collins and Routledge & Kegan Paul 1963)

It is well to know something of his thought before
coming to this.

(c) *Psychology and Religion*
Most of Jung's writings on religion are gathered together
in Vol. 11 of the Collected Edition:

Psychology and Religion

One might recommend the three lectures included in
this volume, themselves entitled 'Psychology and Religion' and also 'Answer to Job', included here but published separately as well (Hodder & Stoughton 1965).
'Answer to Job' is only really comprehensible to one
who already has an understanding of and a sympathy
with Jung's approach to religion.

(d) *Psychology and Alchemy*
The shortest and most concise account of the association
between the ideas of the alchemists and Analytical
Psychology is 'The Psychology of the Transference'
found in:

The Practice of Psychotherapy, Vol. 16 Collected Edition

More discoursive discussions are found in:

Psychology and Alchemy, Vol. 12. Collected Edition
Mysterium Conjunctionis, Vol. 14. Collected Edition

None of these could properly be described as beginners' books.

(e) *Wider Applications*
Three small books of special interest:

The Interpretation of Nature and the Psyche, Jung and
Pauli (Routledge & Kegan Paul 1955)

Here Jung sets forward his concept of 'Synchronicity', that is the meaningful interrelation of physical and psychical events that appear to have no causal connection—an idea associated with the mystery that we call 'chance'.

Flying Saucers (Routledge & Kegan Paul 1959)

A psychological examination of the accounts of UFOs.

The Secret of the Golden Flower (Lund Humphreys
1950—first published 1931)

An interpretation of an illustrated Chinese text.

3 Other Writers

Zürich has been more prolific than London in producing books and much remains untranslated.

(a) *Myth and Legend*

The Origin and Development of Consciousness, Erich
Neumann (Pantheon Books 1954)

The Great Mother, Erich Neumann (Pantheon Books 1955)

The latter began as a commentary on a collection of ancient paintings, figures and statues and developed into a major examination of the archetype of the Great Mother.

The Grail Legend, Anna Jung and Marie Louise von Franz (Hodder & Stoughton 1971)

(b) *Ethics*

There has not been a great deal of sustained writing about ethics from a psychological point of view for a fairly obvious reason. It is most unfortunate that

Depth Psychology and a New Ethic, Erich Neumann (Hodder & Stoughton 1969)

written in 1949, was not translated into English for twenty years.

Suicide and the Soul, James Hillman (Hodder & Stoughton 1964)

deals in part with a specific ethical problem about suicide.

(c) *Religion*

Jung always felt that theologians were too unready to consider and discuss the application of Analytical Psychology to religion, and it is true that, on the whole, Christian theologians seem to have been happier with the ideas of Freud. Two Roman Catholics in this country took a deep interest in his work:

God and the Unconscious, Victor White (Collins and
   Harvill 1952)
Soul and Psyche, Victor White (Collins and Harvill
   1960)
The Water and the Fire, Gerald Vann (Fontana 1961—
   first published 1953)

There are also:

Jung and St. Paul, David Cox (Longmans 1959)
History and Myth, David Cox (Longman, Darton and
   Todd 1961)

Jung and the Problem of Evil, H. L. Philp (Rockliff
   1958)

is of interest, partly as an illustration of the difficulty of
doing justice to Jung's religious ideas if one is not at
home with his general ideas and partly through letters
written by Jung, some to the author and others to me,
published as an appendix.

(d) *Case Studies*
Very few full accounts of an actual analysis are published, for obvious reasons. The only three that come
to mind are the extremely valuable

The Living Symbol, Gerhard Adler

and two by Freudians:

Deep Analysis, Charles Berg (Allen & Unwin 1947)
In the Hands of the Living God, Marion Milner
   (Hogarth Press 1969)

(e) *Papers*

Professional papers are published regularly in

The Journal of Analytical Psychology (the journal of the Society of Analytical Psychology in London)

About five pamphlets each year, a great many written from a jungian point of view, are published by

The Guild of Pastoral Psychology

and past issues are kept in print.

TEACH YOURSELF BOOKS

DEPRESSION
Understanding a Common Problem

C. A. H. Watts

One of the most commonplace problems in every doctor's surgery is that of depression. The suffering caused by attacks of depression is sometimes not appreciated by the sufferer's family or friends, and yet depression is one of the most widespread complaints in modern society—and accounts for the prescribing of immense quantities of drugs by doctors.

This book acts as a guide as to what most frequently causes depression and to what the sufferer can do to come to grips with it. Dr Watts also describes the vital role friends and relatives can perform to relieve the victim's suffering and how they can come to understand and support the sufferer through periods of depression. Doctors, nurses, social workers and students will also find this an explicit and clear guide to the problems of depression and it is hoped that this book will help all those whose lives are touched upon by this painful and increasingly common problem.

ISBN 0 340 19502 9

TEACH YOURSELF BOOKS

SCHIZOPHRENIA
What It Means

A. R. K. Mitchell

One person in every hundred of the population in the United Kingdom will suffer from schizophrenia before the age of forty-five; one in every four of National Health Service beds is occupied by a schizophrenic; and several times the number in hospital have been diagnosed as schizophrenics but are living at home.

Schizophrenia can cause the most acute suffering for the victim, his family and friends. To become a schizophrenic is to become a new person in a new world. The object of this book, written by a consultant psychiatrist, is to show something of this to all those whose lives are touched upon by schizophrenia, so that they can come to a closer understanding of what is happening and what they can do to help. Not only friends and relatives but also students, nurses, social workers and doctors will find Dr Mitchell's book a human and practical account of what schizophrenia means, while sufferers themselves will find this book of real value and assistance.

ISBN 0 340 19504 5

TEACH YOURSELF BOOKS

Care and Welfare Series

☐ 19503 7   **ALCOHOLISM—A SOCIAL DISEASE**   80p
Max Glatt

☐ 19501 0   **CARING FOR THE BABY**   95p
James W. Partridge

☐ 19502 9   **DEPRESSION—UNDERSTANDING A COMMON PROBLEM**   70p
C. A. H. Watts

☐ 19504 5   **SCHIZOPHRENIA—WHAT IT MEANS**   70p
A. R. K. Mitchell

☐ 20768 X   **UNDERSTANDING MENTAL ILLNESS**   95p
Mary Applebey

All these books are available at your local bookshop or newsagent, or can be ordered direct from the publisher. Just tick the titles you want and fill in the form below.

Prices and availability subject to change without notice.

TEACH YOURSELF BOOKS, P.O. Box 11, Falmouth, Cornwall.

Please send cheque or postal order, and allow the following for postage and packing:

U.K.—One book 22p plus 10p per copy for each additional book ordered, up to a maximum of 82p.

B.F.P.O. and EIRE—22p for the first book plus 10p per copy for the next 6 books, thereafter 4p per book.

OTHER OVERSEAS CUSTOMERS—30p for the first book and 10p per copy for each additional book.

Name ....

Address ....

....